PRESENTING
FOR TV AND SCREEN

The Essential Guide

Brian Naylor

PRESENTING
FOR TV AND SCREEN

The Essential Guide

THE CROWOOD PRESS

First published in 2021 by
The Crowood Press Ltd
Ramsbury, Marlborough
Wiltshire SN8 2HR

enquiries@crowood.com

www.crowood.com

British Library Cataloguing-in-Publication Data
A catalogue record for this book is available from the British Library.

ISBN 978 1 78500 951 8

Typeset by Simon and Sons

Cover design by Maggie Mellett

Printed and bound in India by Parksons Graphics Pvt. Ltd.

CONTENTS

ACKNOWLEDGEMENTS   6

PREFACE   7

INTRODUCTION   11

1 EFFECTIVE AND ENGAGING COMMUNICATION   15

2 THE PERFORMANCE OF A PRESENTER   25

3 TV AND VIDEO PRESENTING TECHNIQUES   39

4 TOOLS OF THE TRADE   61

5 INTERVIEWING   85

6 PIECE TO CAMERA (PTC)   97

7 SHOW FORMATS AND PRODUCTION CREW   105

8 CAREER STRATEGY   123

GLOSSARY AND JARGON   152

ONLINE RESOURCES   156

INDEX   157

ACKNOWLEDGEMENTS

Many thanks to all my professional colleagues and friends who have contributed content and images to help make this book possible. Contributing presenters, directors, agents, models and casting professionals include: Annabelle Knight, Ant Webb, Gemma-Leigh James, Karen Witchalls-Plunkett, Octavia Alexandru, Ruth Warrilow and Sam Darlaston.

I would particularly like to thank Helen Sheppard, not only for her contribution but also for her ongoing support and involvement in The TV Training Academy.

My gratitude and thanks also go to Abby Aron for her expertise and help with the editorial.

PREFACE

Understand that failure is not the opposite of success, it's part of success.

(Arianna Huffington)

A couple of decades ago, when working as a freelance presenter, I landed a job with a company that ran TV presenting courses. On the first day I sat in on one of my new colleague's training sessions, in order to get a sense of how things were done.

My colleague was working with a young man, getting him to imagine that he was broadcasting live from outside a rave. He was not explaining clearly what he wanted the young trainee to do and seemed more interested in the camera and lighting equipment than he did in directing or guiding the novice presenter. Even I was confused, and I had done my fair share of outside broadcasting.

Just before the camera began to roll, the young trainee said, 'Excuse me, but I don't understand what it is that you want me to do?'

Instead of explaining his requirements in a coherent way, my colleague simply turned to the young lad and in a condescending voice replied, 'Look, you've either got it or you haven't.'

Luckily, the studio lights were low so no one could see my jaw drop.

That simple phrase, 'You've either got it or you haven't', went on to change the course of my life. I knew that statement simply was not true. To be fair to the director, his experience of working in television would have conditioned him into thinking 'time is money'. In a television studio, there are rarely any spare minutes to start training or nurturing new presenters, or 'talent', as they are often referred to. This belief inspired me to devise my own TV presenter training programme, to provide new talent with the techniques, skills and confidence needed to turn up to a TV studio and deliver a performance.

How can I be so certain that anyone can present, as long as they are given the right guidance? Because I am living, breathing, proof of the fact. Aged 17, I was full of life. Like most young men, I enjoyed joking around, but what I dreaded perhaps more than anything else on earth was having to communicate with anyone I did not know, especially on the telephone. I was unable speak up in a group of people and, if the focus of attention was ever on me, I would feel myself blushing and my heart pounding. The thought of 'public speaking' literally sent shivers down my spine.

Aged 19, I concluded that this introverted behaviour around strangers would severely limit my chances of achieving any of my life goals. There was nothing else for it: I had to face the enormous challenge head on. So, when I saw an advert for 'Holiday Reps' in the paper, I applied and, with the help of my older sister, who was already working in the tourism industry, I managed to impress someone enough to give me a job. I found myself working in Spain as a tour rep for Thomson Holidays.

As a key part of the job, I was required to present Thomson's range of activities and trips to an audience of holidaymakers, not once, but five times a week. I was so terrified about the prospect that I was packing my bags for home on a near daily basis.

When it came to my turn to perform, I was shockingly bad. My supervisor walked out halfway through one of my first presentations, shaking his head, and I remember thinking, 'OK, that is it, my time working within the tourism industry is over.'

A short time later, I was relocated to a larger hotel, with a team of more experienced tour reps. With their guidance and encouragement, I was able to pull off my presentations, not only the first time but the second and all subsequent times. After several successful 'performances', my confidence began to grow as I discovered that I had a knack for engaging with a crowd. In turn, this spurred me on to improving my methods for hooking my audience in.

A few months later, a twist of fate led to me having to step in at the last minute for one of the Thomson nightly entertainers, who had broken a bone in their foot playing football. With barely a moment to think, I found myself in the spotlight, and was amazed to discover that I loved every minute of it. The positive feedback from the audience led me to my decision to forge a career as a performer. With this is mind, when the summer season ended, I headed to London, with the aim of becoming a TV presenter.

A year later I found myself back in Spain, with a job as an entertainer in the holiday hotels. I had spent my time in London working in call centres and bars and as a delivery driver, but had done very little in the way of presenting. I could not understand why, after such great feedback from the hotel audiences, I had not been discovered, so I had headed back abroad to massage my bruised ego. This was one of the many mistakes I have made over my presenting career: blaming other people for my own shortcomings.

Another holiday season came to an end in Spain, and we began to prepare for the next. A new management team took over the entertainment, and I found myself working with an experienced director called Tom. He had worked in Hollywood, the West End and on television, and he was the one who gave me my first professional industry feedback: 'Hate to break it to you, Brian,' he said, 'but you're not a great presenter.'

Ouch.

Painful as it was to hear, this damning assessment taught me a great lesson: friends, family and holidaymakers spending a few weeks in the sun will all give you positive feedback because they like you, but in the wider world it does not count for much.

'You could be good,' Tom went on to say, 'but you need to get professional training. Learn to use your voice and get familiar with the tools needed to present.'

What I had hoped was that someone in the industry would spot my talent and invest their time and effort in me, when I had not even bothered to invest my time in my own development. This was a turning point for me. I promptly resigned and headed back to London.

I filled every spare moment I had building my presenting career and it was hard work. I attended every presenting course I could find, along with some acting courses. I took on a number of student projects and I worked for free. Carving out a successful living as a presenter requires commitment, dedication, astuteness, tenacity and, most of all, a thick skin. Every moment of toil was worth it.

Fast forward ten years and I was working in front of 10,000 people at Wembley Arena. I was also presenting live TV and even having a go at stand-up comedy. As I said before, I am living proof that everyone, even the shyest human being on earth, can present.

I have loved many aspects of my presenting and training career as every contract is different. I have travelled the world, met people from all walks of life and watched hundreds of trainees step up to the mark and set forth on highly successful careers of their own. I truly believe that, with effective and engaging communication skills, professional training and an unstoppable attitude, everyone has the potential to achieve great results.

This book is a culmination of my many years of experience presenting, directing and running the TV Training Academy. Its purpose is to give you all the techniques, tips, insights and practical skills you need in order to become a TV or video presenter, so that you can go confidently into the increasingly big wide world of opportunity. Do not be one of the many who sit back waiting for their presenting dreams to come true; sitting back is not going to make it happen. Seize the day and make your dreams a reality because, regardless of what anyone tells you, you have got what it takes.

DIFFICULT
ROADS
LEAD TO
BEAUTIFUL
DESTINATIONS

INTRODUCTION

The harder I work the luckier I am.

(Jack Nicholson, Hollywood actor)

One of the greatest features of TV and video presenting is that anyone *can* do it. Seriously. There are no hard and fast rules or qualifications required and no career ladder that is set in stone. In fact, there are endless potential ways of getting into the industry. So, if you want to be a TV presenter, a YouTuber or maybe you just need to present videos for a work project, this book can help you become a professional on-screen communicator. It will provide you with all the insights, techniques and professional tips that will help you communicate effectively on camera. It will cover all the inside knowledge and know-how for getting work and, from there, help you develop a career strategy so that you can take advantage of all the possibilities that are out there waiting for you.

If, however, you are looking to become an overnight 'star' through becoming a presenter, you might be in for a shock. There are far easier ways to become rich and famous. Think of all the politicians, sportspeople, entrepreneurs, authors, astronauts and chefs – the list goes on – who have achieved fame and fortune and are now house-hold names. Almost every industry and sector has its fair share of notably successful people and generally the only common theme is that they have all worked hard, and have been focused and 100 per cent committed. Working as a TV or YouTube presenter is no different from engaging in any other profession. It can take years to build a career, but with a little bit of hard work and practice anyone can significantly improve their on-screen communication and increase their chances of achieving that success.

As with other professions, there are certain characteristics that will stand a person in good stead in their search for success. They may have a particular level of expertise, like the physicist Brian Cox. They may be endowed with bundles of natural energy and enthusiasm, like the historian Dr Lucy Worsley. They might be particularly calm under pressure or excellent at communicating. Maybe they have a very thick skin. Being in the public eye or even just posting videos on a social media channel often attracts unwelcome feedback that can be very upsetting, especially if you are sensitive to criticism. Anyone can air their views on an online forum with complete anonymity and as a result comments are often disproportionately harsh.

NEVER A BETTER TIME

With a myriad of TV stations and new streaming platforms launching on an almost monthly basis, this is a heyday time for TV and video presenters. A recent poll by global research company TNS of 55,000 internet users found that 75 per cent of the worldwide population still watch television as their main form of entertainment. Admittedly, many people watch multiple screens at the same time, so presenters need to work doubly hard to keep their audience's attention. However, that audience is a global one, made up of a huge number of digitally connected citizens, so there are no limits on the range of opportunities available in presenting.

Some of the unforgiving criticism of presenters may be down to a common assumption that they have an easy job. This is because, when it is done well, it appears that they are simply chatting to their audience. Few people are aware of the skills and talent needed to achieve these results. It is only when things are not done well that it becomes noticeable; at that point, the seamless illusion is broken.

One vital personality trait that is needed by a presenter to achieve the illusion of 'chatting' is confidence. Being well prepared, knowing what to expect and understanding studio terminology and equipment goes a long way in building that confidence, but the most important thing is a belief in your own ability. If a presenter doubts themselves or is nervous, the audience will associate that doubt with what is being said and assume that the speaker does not know what they are talking about. Although this may be a million miles from the truth, as soon as the audience loses trust in a presenter, they may simply turn off. When that happens, all is lost.

This book is set out in a way that will give you an in-depth understanding of how effective communication is achieved. It will show you how best to adapt that communication to 'fit' the screen using performance and technique. Following on from this, it will cover the 'tools of the trade', such as teleprompters, talkback, interviewing and working to time, before providing you with all the inside knowledge and know-how for breaking into the wide world of TV and video presenting. Expect to find career strategies, tips for meeting producers face-to-face, business plans, interview hints and advice for putting across your best audition.

Learning how to present is only a small part of the presenting journey. The real work begins when you start putting everything provided in this book into practice. Desire, drive and ambition is what will set you apart from the many thousands of 'wannabes', who let the dream escape their grasp.

Although this book will provide all the practical knowledge, as well as offering routes and advice for going forward and forging a career, you do need to bear in mind that this is a tough industry to crack and the competition is fierce. If you are to become one of the few who achieve success, that will be down to you, but you should never forget that you have as much right to be a part of it as anyone else. If there is such a thing as a good time to be cutting your teeth in a rich, diverse, burgeoning industry, that time is now.

Good luck!

The more time and effort you invest into developing your presentation skills, the quicker your on-screen confidence and talent appear.

1
EFFECTIVE AND ENGAGING COMMUNICATION

Communication comes naturally to human beings. From the moment a baby draws its first breath and lets out that cry, it is communicating, and will continue to communicate at varying levels of effectiveness throughout the course of its life. It is no wonder then that communication is often cited as the most important life skill a person can possess. It is our means of acquiring knowledge, of progressing, of asking for help and, on an extreme level, our survival may depend on it.

In the vast majority of job adverts, 'excellent communication skills' are listed as an essential requirement. Employers know that those who are good at expressing themselves in an articulate way have a far greater chance of succeeding in the workplace. It goes without saying that the ability to communicate well is at the top of every aspiring presenter's tick list, because it is pivotal to their purpose. Presenters who are unable to communicate are as effective as doctors who are scared at the sight of blood. It is therefore helpful to understand the different elements that are at work when people communicate with each other.

WHAT IS COMMUNICATION?

The word 'communicate' comes from the Latin *communicare*, which means 'to share'. In its simplest form, the process of communication consists of three main elements:

1. The *sender* who generates and imparts a message.
2. The *channel* through which the information is conveyed.
3. The *recipient* receiving the message and decoding it.

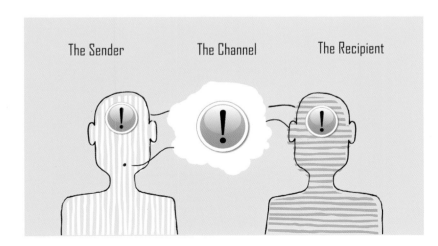

The Sender   The Channel   The Recipient

The sender generates a message that is sent via the channel (words, tonality and visual signals), to be interpreted by the receiver.

The TV or video presenter is in the position of sender, as they are generating the message to send. The channel through which they are imparting their message is their speech and/or expressions. The recipient is the viewer. The channel should be a presenter's main concern and a full, in-depth understanding of how it works is a distinct advantage for a communicator.

THREE-DIMENSIONAL COMMUNICATION

When formulating words, sentences and questions, the sender's main focus is on the message they want to convey. For example, when they say, 'Would you like to go out for dinner with me?', in their mind, they are thinking about their desire or need. The words, expressions, tone of voice and movements that convey that need are formed largely on a subconscious level. The recipient hears the words, but is also aware of the tone of voice in which the message is being imparted, and is watching the way the sender looks as they say it. They use all three factors to ascertain the meaning or intent of the invitation. Is the 'dinner' just an opportunity to eat and discuss work, or is the offer something more complex, multi-layered and potentially romantic?

Only by taking into account all three dimensions – words, tone of voice and visual signals – can the recipient properly interpret the sender's true intention. A presenter is in the position of sender, but very often they have interrupted the natural process of formulating messages, by removing any need or desire and consciously preparing the words they are going to say. It is no wonder, then, that first-time presenters can feel awkward and nervous. If the normal desire or need to communicate a message has been replaced by consciously scripted words and an unnatural feeling, this is what will be formulated on a subconscious level and this is what the recipient will receive.

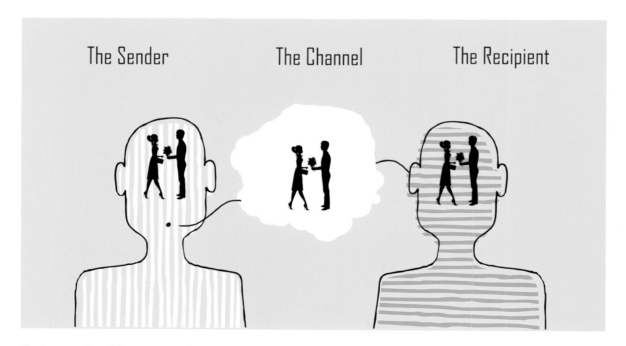

The Sender   The Channel   The Recipient

The true meaning of the message – the intention, sentiment and feeling – is carried mainly in subtle tonal and visual signals.

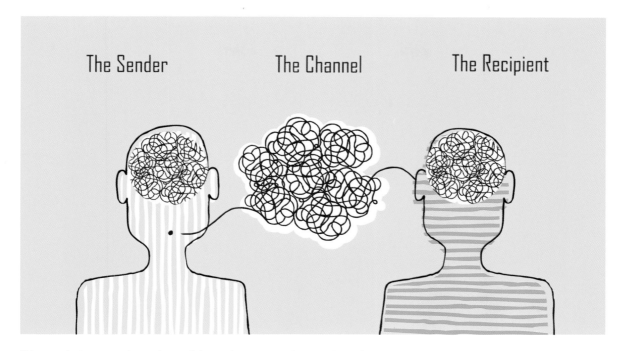

The Sender   The Channel   The Recipient

If the sender has no real meaning, or is just trying to remember a script and get the words out in the right order, the tonal and visual signals will conflict with the words being said.

Part of the job of a presenter is to make it as easy as possible for the viewer or listener to understand the message. Sending awkward, unnatural signals gets in the way of that process, so it is vital to eliminate any of those and master the art of formulating consciously prepared messages and scripts. To do that requires an understanding of the concept of three-dimensional communication.

PARALINGUISTICS

In the late 1960s and early 1970s, Professor of Psychology Albert Mehrabian, from the University of California, conducted a number of studies into the ways in which different forms of communication imparted by the sender are interpreted by the receiver. One of these studies dealt with paralinguistics, which is defined in the Oxford Dictionary as 'communication through ways other than words, for example tone of voice, expressions on the face and actions'. From his findings, Mehrabian formulated what has become known as the 7-38-55 Rule. This states that only 7 per cent of the underlying meaning, the feel or intent of what we communicate occurs by way of the words, while 38 per cent comes through tone of voice, or tonality as it is known, and 55 per cent through visual signals such as facial expressions and body language.

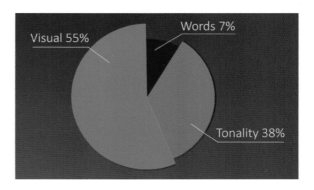

The true or underlying meaning of what is being said is carried in facial expressions, body language and tonality.

The way in which Mehrabian conducted his research has been the subject of much criticism over the years. However, the concepts offer some useful insights into and understanding of the importance that presenters should place on the different aspects on non-verbal communication.

Words (7 Per Cent)

If you are new to presenting, chances are you are going to find yourself overly focusing on the words you choose to say. You might worry that you will miss out words, forget the lines or lose your place. You might worry that your tongue will freeze, and you will not be able to get the words out, or that you will be judged for what you say.

These are all very natural worries that tie in with ten greatest fears public speakers have:

- Fear of being judged.
- Fear of coming across as stupid.
- Fear of being 'found out', aka imposter syndrome.
- Fear of making a mistake.
- Fear of forgetting what to say.
- Fear of freezing or becoming-tongue tied.
- Fear of saying something politically incorrect.

What is interesting about the words, however, is that they prove effective only if they are in alignment with the *way* you say them, and the way you 'come across' *as* you say them. If you do not believe the words you are saying, or you are unsure of yourself or unclear about what they mean, you will not be able to deliver the words in a convincing way, as your unconscious communication, tone of voice, facial expressions and body language will let you down. The viewer will become preoccupied by what you are *not* saying as opposed to by the words coming out through your lips. It is for this reason that being comfortable and well-practised with the words and messages makes all the difference to how you come across when you present.

Tonality (38 Per Cent)

Everyone has had the experience of sitting through a talk, class, lesson or speech, where they are a captive audience for a speaker droning on (and on), to the extent that all they can do is keep their eyes on the clock and will the time to speed up. The main reason for this sense of tedium is generally a lack of any variation in the tonality of the speaker's voice.

Tonality is the way you *sound* when you speak and is determined by your volume, pitch, pace and rhythm. Making adjustments to any of these individual aspects of tonality can completely change the meaning of the words. Take the simple sentence, 'It is really great to be here.' First, try saying the sentence with an upbeat pace, mid-to-high tone and a good variety of pitch, placing strong emphasis on the 'really' and the 'great'. Second, try the same phrase but with a low pitch, in a monotone and slow.

The first example is more likely to sound as though it is genuinely meant and that it is actually *really great* to be there. The second may well be interpreted as sarcastic, bored or cynical, changing the feeling and therefore the meaning of the message.

Your tone of voice can help the viewer ascertain whether you are being serious or fun, teasing or genuine, worked up or calm. People who are new to presenting often lack the confidence to 'play' with their voice and see what they can do with it to create maximum impact. At first, they will tend to keep the voice within a narrow tonal range as this will be their comfort zone, where they feel safest. The problem with keeping the tone of your voice at one level is that it runs the risk of sounding monotonal.

The very word, 'monotonal', implies the flat mood it creates. When the range of tone is limited to just one level, the audience will perceive the presentation as repetitive and so tend to switch off and stop listening. Nine times out of ten, a speaker who has the ability to engage with an audience will be doing so not only because of the words they say but also because of the way they are expressing them. They will work their voice to emphasize certain points; they may pause, increase volume, decrease volume, raise the tone, lower the tone. All these have an enormous impact on the quality of the presentation. You can have the punchiest, most amusing, hard-hitting words to impart, but if you recite them in a flat deadbeat way, your audience will not stick around.

One way of improving the range of your pitch is to practise vocal exercises in advance of your presentation. Starting on 'Ah', sing the notes up and down the scale. Prepare the words you intend to say in advance by highlighting areas of emphasis and changes in tone. Reading your words aloud several times beforehand is also useful. Through familiarity, you become more comfortable with what you are saying and become better able to add colour and style.

Visual Signals (55 Per Cent)

Most people have some kind of daily interaction with another human being, so generally they are pretty well practised at reading facial expressions and body language. Through this, they can tell what someone is thinking, as well as reading their emotions to assess the nature of the thought – is it happy, sad, worried or excited? They may very quickly work out whether someone is about to laugh or cry, and they are pretty attuned to recognizing surprise, disgust, horror, and so on.

Let us go back to that simple phrase, 'It is really great to be here.' Initially, you might think that, with a sentence such as this, there is no room for confusion. True, if it is said with warmth, enthusiasm, open body language and a genuine smile, then its sincerity need not be doubted. If, on the other hand, it is said with a frown, closed body language and no eye contact, the perceived meaning of the phrase can change. This is because the true dynamic, feel or intent of the phrase lies predominantly in the visual signals that are subconsciously being transmitted by the speaker. Someone watching and listening will respond most to the biggest percentage of the three dimensions of communication. If the speaker is succeeding in getting the words out correctly (7 per cent), with the appropriate tone of voice (38 per cent), but their visual signals (55 per cent) are reflecting a conflicting message, it is the latter that the audience will pick up on. It is vital to align tonality, visual signals and words, so that they are all sending a congruent message, thus making it easy for the audience to understand.

THE POWER OF FACIAL EXPRESSIONS IN POLITICS

It would not be far off the mark to say that the media has the power to make or break a person, depending on their body language. During the 2008 presidential debate featuring Senator John McCain and Senator Barack Obama, McCain's inability to make eye contact with Obama was interpreted by the media as him 'looking down his nose' at his opponent. In the 1976 US presidential election, research by Friedman, Di Matteo and Mertz found that news presenters displayed more favourable facial expressions (nods of the head, smiles, relaxed reporting) when discussing candidate Jimmy Carter than they did when talking about his rival Gerald Ford (blinking, head thrusting, more aggressive stance). Other studies found news presenters showing positive facial expressions when discussing Ronald Reagan over Walter Mondale, and a correlation between viewers' choice of candidates and the TV news channels that they watched.

FACIAL EXPRESSIONS THE WORLD OVER

There is widespread support for the theory that there are six basic emotions, which, when genuinely expressed, use the same set of facial muscles among all human beings. In 1969, Professor Paul Ekman travelled the world studying the connection between facial expressions and emotions. Focusing on five different cultures – from Chile, Argentina, Brazil, Japan and the United States – he discovered that the facial expressions reflecting anger, disgust, fear, happiness, sadness and surprise are universally recognizable. He also found that it takes an observer less than one-twenty-fifth of a second to determine what an expression means and whether it is genuine.

Facial expressions are an important part of communication as they express sentiment, feeling and underlying meaning. They are also the way an observer judges an individual's reaction to what they are saying.

One area of concern for Ekman centred on whether the expressions were learnt or inherent. He was aware that all the participants had access to television and magazines, and that they might simply be recognizing the expressions through being exposed to them. In order to eliminate this possibility, he travelled to a remote part of Papua New Guinea to work with an isolated tribe called the Fore, who had never been exposed to Western civilization. He found that this remote group of people recognized the various facial expressions in the same way as their Western counterparts. The studies were then repeated with test subjects who were blind from birth; again, the same results were recorded. Clearly, human beings are proficient at reading emotions and adept at recognizing when facial expressions are being forced or fake.

The following pictures show the difference between some genuine and insincere expressions, where the facial muscles have been either used subconsciously or deliberately manipulated. If you can identify the 'fakes', you, like the vast majority of the population, are an expert at reading facial expressions. When a fellow human being tries to produce an expression by manipulating the muscles in their face, most observers will instantly read them as insincere. The mouth may be smiling but the eyes remain expressionless. This is the 'cheesy' smile that anyone with an ability to read facial expressions will straight away identify as disingenuous.

The orbicularis oculi muscles around the eyes contract when a person smiles in a sincere way.

The orbicularis oculi muscles are largely controlled on a subconscious level, so they are not engaged by a smile that is not genuine.

Certain feelings such as sadness, anger and concern can be reflected in very subtle facial expressions, as the person is often trying to hide them.

Pulling a face to express an emotion in acting is known as 'ham' acting and can be comical.

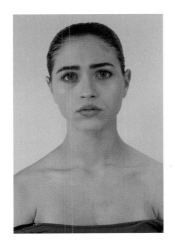

The eyes are the windows to the soul. If you believe it or genuinely feel it, your audience will be able to see it in your eyes and expressions.

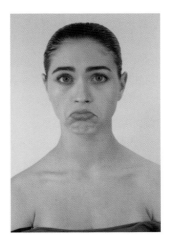

When a person makes a conscious effort to manipulate the muscles in their face to express an emotion, the results are often exaggerated and come across as artificial.

BODY LANGUAGE CAN SPEAK LOUDER THAN WORDS

How many times have you thought to yourself, 'I don't believe a word that man says'? You may not have noticed anything particularly suspect in what he is saying, but on a subconscious level you may have spotted a bouncy knee, fiddly hands or a repetitive shift of weight from one leg to the other. These almost imperceptible modifications may leave you with a feeling or perhaps just a vibe that something is not quite right. This is body language communicating from behind the scenes of the words being spoken.

The phrase 'gut reaction' refers to the bodily response that gives us an indication of whether to trust in somebody or something. 'It just does not feel quite right,' we often say, when instinct tells us to be suspicious. Every time the brain triggers an emotion to play out in a facial expression, it also triggers a response in the gut or, more delicately, the digestive system, which can reflect every kind of feeling. Where the facial muscles register as angry, the digestive system constricts, increasing the production of acid, which slows down digestion and produces an element of discomfort. Equally, fear will cause the digestive system to feel as though it is tying itself in knots.

First impressions of another person are often picked up by way of the gut – maybe just a feeling, again. It will initially be mirrored in our facial expressions, but these can be adjusted quickly to register neutrality. However, the feeling in the gut may linger.

If the viewer feels 'safe' in the hands of a presenter, they will be able to sit back and listen to what they have to say. However, if there is any element of discomposure on the presenter's behalf, the audience will pick up on this and the words will be lost. Body language is an important topic when learning presenting techniques (*see* Chapter 3).

As viewers and listeners become increasingly adept at multitasking, it is all the more essential for a presenter to impart their message in an engaging, authentic manner. They must ensure that all three dimensions of communication are aligned, so that the viewer is given the full opportunity to receive and interpret the message loudly and clearly.

VOCAL TECHNIQUES AND EXERCISES

Breathing

Although breathing is pivotal to our ability to communicate, it is often overlooked. This is most likely because, whether we actively think about our breathing or not, we still breathe, so that we have a tendency to take it for granted. The power we exert in the voice is, however, completely dependent on the quality of the sound that we produce, which is in turn dependent on the breath.

When we are relaxed, breath flows freely through our lungs. Conversely, anxiety creates tension and tightens the throat, forcing us to strain our voice, so that the sound comes out high-pitched. One of the best ways of relaxing the throat is to yawn, allowing the jaw to drop as far as is comfortable.

Where we breathe from is also pivotal to the power of the voice – again, anxiety forces us to breathe from the upper chest, which also constricts the voice. However, consciously breathing deeply is not necessarily the answer. The body uses deep breaths as a way of preparing for the fight or flight response, so taking too many deep breaths will actually increase anxiety. The key is to control the breathing.

One way to help the body relax and to get a hold of any nerves before a presentation is to lengthen the exhalation, following a simple breathing pattern of 4-7-8. Inhale normally for four seconds, hold the breath for seven seconds and exhale for eight seconds. This can be repeated up to four times.

When presenting, taking breaths that feel like they are travelling up from the belly enables you to draw much more air into your lungs. You need to be able to feel your belly rise on the inhalation and fall on the exhalation. Breathing in this way adds gravitas, depth and strength to the voice. It is more pleasant on the ear of the listener and adds more authority to the message being imparted.

Voice Confrontation

Are you one of those people who hears their voice on a recording and winces? If this is you, you are not alone. In fact, it is such a common reaction that there is a phrase for it: 'voice confrontation'. The reason we often cringe at the sound of our own voice is because it sounds completely different from how we *think* it sounds. When we speak, we hear two slightly different versions of our voice: the external sound that everyone else hears and an internal sound or vibration that make its way from the vocal box through the head before reaching the inner ears. The internal sound is often perceived to be lower in tone, due to the dampening effect of the bones and flesh of the head. As a result, we are accustomed to hearing our voice as richer or smoother than it actually is.

After confronting your recorded voice multiple times, you will get used to it, but for the first few times it can sound 'squeaky' or child-like. Rest assured, unless you have been told that you have an issue, or you are aware of one, your voice sounds perfectly fine. It is actually useful to listen to how you sound, as it will provide you with a new perspective and help you to adjust it accordingly.

Enunciation

You can spend endless hours preparing the best script, but if you do not articulate the words clearly when presenting, you may as well not have got out of bed. Once upon a time, only one type of voice was considered appropriate for presenting:

the clipped and plummy 'Received Pronunciation' (RP), also known as 'the Queen's English'. If you want to be reminded of how this sounded, go back and listen to old radio footage from news anchors reporting on the Second World War. Fortunately, things have moved on from those days, so that regional accents and all forms of English are now commonplace. In fact, nowadays regional accents are not only acceptable, but in some situations they are actively sought after – as long as they are easily understandable.

HELEN SHEPPARD: DIRECTOR'S SUMMARY

Presenting is all about communication. However strange it may seem talking to a camera, it is essential to use everything you have at your disposal. Even the dullest subject can be made to sound fascinating if your body language, facial expression and tone of voice work together. Enthusing your audience with your voice can make a huge difference. A small facial expression can say so much. It is your body language that brings your words to life.

COMMUNICATION AT A GLANCE

There are three dimensions of communication: words, tonality, visual signals.

- Tonality and visual signals play a significant role in conveying the meaning or sentiment of what is being said.
- Manipulating the facial muscles to simulate emotion is 'cheesy' presenting.
- All three dimensions of communication should be used, to make it easy for the person listening to understand the message.

2
THE PERFORMANCE OF A PRESENTER

When a presenter comes across to the viewer as comfortable and confident, they are easy to watch. This is because human beings have the ability to empathize. If someone appears awkward and unsure, we feel uncomfortable on their behalf. Similarly, if someone looks like they are at ease in themselves, we are relaxed. It takes a few seconds for viewers to decide whether or not to engage or disengage with whatever or whoever is on their screens. If they are made to feel uncomfortable or unsure, they will not hesitate to switch channels. It is the job of the presenter, therefore, to keep the viewer tuned in and focused on the content without any distractions or concerns.

Once you understand the various elements involved in communication, you can start to look at the different performance techniques and how best to build a bond with the viewer.

WHY DO PEOPLE WATCH TV?

We have all probably enjoyed watching a politician squirm uncomfortably on a current affairs programme, or a celebrity trying to avoid questions about a new romance, or maybe just our favourite presenters attempting not to laugh about something silly. Whatever we enjoy watching, we all like to get a sense of how the people involved feel about what is being said. What do they really think about the person they are interviewing and do they wholeheartedly agree with the comments being made? To reiterate, sentiment, underlying meaning or 'sub-text' cannot be conveyed as easily by words alone. These elements of communication are picked up on a subconscious level via tonality, facial expressions and body language.

Watching television or an online video allows the viewer to consume content in an easily accessible and passive way, as well as getting a 'feel' for the people involved.

One reason we like to know how people feel about what is being said is because it allows us to assess whether they are a similar type of person to us. Do they have similar morals or a sense of humour akin to our own? Put simply, are they a friend? Relationships are built on trust and rapport. We like people who we feel are similar to us or people whom we admire or want to emulate. It is easier to ascertain whether someone is our type of person by watching them speak than by reading about them.

The most sought-after presenters are often those whom the viewer does not see as a 'personality' but as a friend – someone they could get along with. This is because the presenter, by communicating openly and honestly, has enabled the viewer to put their trust in them and build a rapport. Sometimes, the trust is such that the viewer may be disappointed by the presenter, in the same way as they would with a friend. This can happen when the personal life of a presenter is thrust into the spotlight, revealing an aspect of their life that the viewer did not know about. Viewers often claim to feel 'let down' in these cases, unhappy that they had not been privy to every part of the presenter's personal life. When this happens, it is clear that the presenter has succeeded in communicating on an empathic level with the viewer.

If a presenter is putting on an act, is too nervous to show any emotions or is just not very expressive, it is hard for the viewer to make a connection. Directors like to work with presenters who are open and have a quality that is known as 'vulnerability'. This does not refer to someone who is physically weak or at risk, nor does it imply that they are mentally susceptible. It simply means that they are not afraid to let their guard down and be themselves. As Oscar Wilde said, 'Be yourself. Everyone else is already taken.' It sounds easy, doesn't it? After all, who else are you going to be? In truth, though, it is not as easy to be yourself in front of a camera as you might think. Very often, people who are warm, easy-going and the life and soul of the party change the moment they look into the lens. They become formal and stiff, adopting behaviours more suited to meeting a lofty official than a friend in a coffee shop. This often happens to new presenters because they are holding back from being their true selves. Their defence mechanisms are kicking in to protect the delicate ego inside. After all, no one really wants to be told they are not very good or, worse, that they are disliked

If you are your true, authentic self, like-minded people will gravitate towards your video content and you will be able to build a fan base or 'tribe'.

by other people. It can feel safer to hide away your personality, feelings and opinions. In that way, any criticism is not a personal affront but, instead, only affects the person you are pretending to be. To be a good presenter, however, you will need to be courageous and sufficiently confident to reveal the real person inside. By letting your guard down and allowing people to 'see' the real you, and have an understanding of your thoughts, feelings and opinions, you will attract the right audience. These people are sometimes referred to as a presenter's 'tribe'.

CHARM AND CHARISMA

The two personality traits of charm and charisma tend to go together because, when someone comes across as charismatic, the charm shines through. The Cambridge Dictionary describes charisma as 'a special power that some people have naturally that makes them able to influence other people and attract their attention and admiration'. This 'special power' sounds perfect for a presenter, so how can you acquire it? Charismatic people are either born with the capacity to be themselves without any hang-ups or insecurities, or have mastered the skills to be this way. They are comfortable in their own skin and they trust their own opinions and thoughts. If you want to be a presenter, you should too. Your beliefs, judgement and approach to different situations are what set you apart and you should celebrate your difference, as it is your biggest selling point as a presenter. Your opinions and beliefs are all subjective and depend on your personal experiences – what you have read, whom you have spoken to and situations you have witnessed. Not everyone will agree with your approach or ideology, but that should not be a problem. As long as you are genuine, fair and considerate and, very importantly, you have nothing to hide, you will be OK.

One important thing to note is that a charismatic person is not trying to please everyone all the time. Neediness does not feature in their thought process. They are not motivated by a need to be liked and they are not trying to impress anyone. In general, trying too hard implies desperation, and that is not an attractive trait. You should not, however, confuse trying too hard with working hard. A professional presenter will have done the hard work well before the show gets under way. Any scripts, agendas or specific show items will have been thoroughly learned and understood. This means that, as soon as the cameras roll, they can come across as relaxed and in control, fully comfortable in front of the camera. This, in turn, allows the audience to relax and enjoy the show.

There is often the assumption that charismatic people are perfect communicators who make no mistakes and produce a seamless presentation every time. This is far from the truth. Charismatic people make just as many mistakes as others, but it is the human way in which they deal with them that sets them apart.

Psychologist Richard Wiseman undertook a study looking at what makes people comes across as charismatic. It involved two female actresses set up to sell blenders in a shopping mall:

Actress 1 gave a seamless presentation and produced a perfect smoothie.
Actress 2 gave a seamless presentation but, in attempting to make the smoothie, forgot to put the lid on the blender, so got covered in its contents.

When the audience were asked to rate the two actresses, Actress 2 came across as more likeable, as her vulnerability humanized her and so made her more relatable. Similar studies have been repeated over and again, always with the same results, highlighting that charisma does not come from being perfect but from a person being true to their human self.

One of the greatest mistakes that an aspiring presenter can make is trying to be someone they are not. They see a presenter they like and think, 'I want to be him', or, 'I'm going to try out the same style as her'. Don't do it. What the television industry is missing right now is *you*. It has never met *you* before and would like to know who *you* are: your opinions, your angles, what it is that makes you tick. This is because the real you, the true you, is totally different from the true anyone else. It is what makes you, you. You, in all your authentic glory, are your unique selling point (USP). There is no one else like you on the whole of planet Earth.

Let that be your inspiration.

It is important to be aware, however, that, when starting out, a new presenter may well gain experience and opportunities from a huge variety of different jobs. Adverts, and corporate or training videos are just some examples of presenting work that do not always require an individual's personal opinions and thoughts to shine through. These roles very often just need a competent presenter who can deliver a message or specific information clearly and professionally. Jobs such as these are a new presenter's 'bread and butter', providing needed practice and experience, as well as money. The reality is that some people are happy to have this type of work to last their entire career. For those who wish to host their own personality-led shows on TV, radio and YouTube, however, it will be essential to learn how to expose their personality.

Rest assured that, if you are just being yourself, people who think like you, are interested in what you have to say, or respect your take on specific subjects will enjoy watching you. It you try to appeal to everyone, you will come across as bland and lacking in character. On top of this, you will find yourself becoming desperately drained. After all, who is 'everyone'? It is overwhelming to constantly attempt to second-guess what millions of people might want.

It could be the case that whatever you have to say, and the way that you say it, happens to appeal to a wide audience, but you should have the courage to let them come to you because of who you are without compromising your authenticity. If you are confident and sure of yourself and the message that you are delivering, you will exude charisma and charm and the audience will naturally gravitate towards you.

ENERGY AND ENTHUSIASM

The only aspect of 'being yourself' that requires any kind of a performance is when it comes to energy and enthusiasm, both of which are crucial to the role of the presenter. Sometimes you might just not be feeling particularly enthusiastic or passionate. Maybe the product you are promoting or reporting on does not excite you, or perhaps you are just having one of those days. The viewer does not need to know any of this; they are unaware that e-bikes are of no interest to you or that you dropped your bag in a puddle on the way to the studio. As far as the viewer is concerned, you are, at the very least, interested in whatever it is you are presenting. If you are not able to show any interest or enthusiasm for your subject matter, neither will your audience.

Of course, no one can be expected to have enthusiasm and passion ticking over at maximum revs 24/7. That would be impossible – and exhausting to watch. It is for this reason that you need to identify mental or physical triggers that get you into the right frame of mind or mood when needed. It might be a healthy bout of butterflies in your belly or the general vibe in the studio, or it might help if you have your own go-to imagined story. You might try to re-create, for example, your delight if you were upgraded from economy to first class on a flight, or if you had bumped into a friend you had not seen for years and were able to enjoy a great catch-up. The increase in energy in those cases would be subtle, and different for everybody. If you are naturally full of energy, you may not need much revving up compared with other, less energized people.

To find the right energy for your on-screen persona, imagine meeting up with a good friend and having an interesting and engaging conversation.

YOU ON A REALLY GOOD DAY

A good way of getting yourself into the right presenting 'mood', is cast your mind back to what you remember as a really great day. Vividly imagine the events and try to recall how you felt. Before too long, some of that happy feeling will rub off on your current mood and you will be on the way to putting yourself in the right frame of mind. The more vividly you can remember or imagine the event, the more impact it will have on your current mood. After some practice, you will be able to turn it on as effortlessly as a light switch.

This is the performance of a presenter. They can create a genuine mood or a feeling in much the same way as an actor might in prepping for a role. It is for this ability to perform that presenters are very often referred to whilst on set as 'talent'.

Using Energy in a Subtle Way

Performing does not, however, mean being constantly at the same energy level. If the subject matter is more serious or there is a call for a more delicate approach, you will need to adapt your delivery, just as you would in the real world. Friends who are exceedingly upbeat 100 per cent of the time can become exhausting to be with, as energy is contagious; too much energy over a long period will exhaust an audience too. Use your energy wisely and try not to be over-enthusiastic about everything. Vary your approach with intrigue, curiosity and/or humour.

If you use your energy to put yourself in the right mood, it will naturally enhance your expressions and intonation. It is this subtle 'lift' that the camera wants to see.

A presenter's level of energy can transform them from being good to being great, but it must be used wisely. The more subtle it is, the more likely it is to excite, enlighten and entertain the viewer. Attempting to energize your presentation by shouting, throwing your arms about and using words such as 'amazing' all the time is a prime example of trying too hard. It is unlikely to be effective. The energy must come from within and knowing how to harness it so that it works for you is what will set you apart from many of your contemporaries.

Adding a Smile

One feeling or mood that a presenter needs to master is warmth. This is the ability to smile or show some affection, in a genuine way. Many TV shows, radio programmes and videos start with the words 'Hello and welcome'. If that line is delivered with an insincere, fake smile, the audience will straight away have a reason not to trust the presenter. After all, if they are prepared to be dishonest about how they feel, what else might they be dishonest about?

The same applies when presenting a radio programme or recording a podcast. A smiling voice has a very obvious tone, which is more pleasing on the ear, and a listening audience is just as adept at hearing false warmth in a voice as a viewing one.

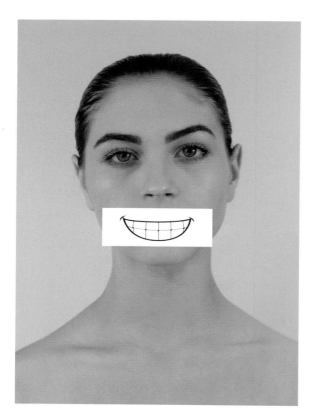

Turning up the corners of your mouth to project a smile is 'cheesy' presenting and is a good way to make an audience mistrust you.

One way of achieving a genuine smile is to use a technique known professionally as the 'knee tickle'. This is something that is taught on the presenting courses at the TV Training Academy. Just before a presenter starts to present, one of the other trainees, just out of shot, tickles their knee. This simple act of silliness makes the presenter relax and smile and they carry that smile into their first words, which are very often 'Hello and welcome'. The audience can see that there is genuine warmth and a sincere smile because there *is* genuine warmth and a sincere smile. What they cannot see, however, is the real reason for the smile. They assume that the warmth and smile are associated with what the presenter is saying, not because the presenter has been tickled, and tricked into a perfectly genuine and natural 'performance'.

This method of getting into an appropriate frame of mind is not always useful on a practical level but it does illustrate how an external stimulus can be used to create the right mood or feeling. A presenter may also use an internal stimulus, such as their imagination, to achieve similar results.

PRESENTING VERSUS ACTING

It may be a contradiction in terms, but the best presenters are not pretending, they are simply *being*! It is not unusual for people unfamiliar with the world of presenting to assume that acting and presenting are one and the same, when in fact they are very different in many ways. An actor takes on the persona, style and mannerisms of someone or something different from themselves. In order to do this, they have to learn how to *be* someone they are not and to play the part in a context that may be out of keeping with their own. Presenting, on the other hand, is all about being yourself. It is not about adopting the characteristics or mannerisms of other people. If a presenter attempts such behaviour, the viewer will pickup on it in an instant and question why they are being fake and what it is that they are hiding. It is for this reason that personality plays a pivotal role when it comes to presenting.

When actors are interacting with other actors they very rarely look directly into the camera – unless, of course, it is in order intentionally to 'break the fourth wall' (as Phoebe Waller-Bridge does in *Fleabag*), which is still done in character. The presenter's main interaction, on the other hand, is with the viewer by way of the camera, with the aim of building rapport. Actors switching to presenting often find this shift in performance tricky. They are so used to being someone else that they can struggle to adapt to being themselves.

There are, of course, always exceptions and occasionally the roles of actor and presenter do cross over. These tend to be comedy roles played by actors; Keith Lemon, Ali G and Dame Edna Everage are a few examples.

COPING WITH NERVES

It is very normal to feel nervous when you first start out. After all, you are in a new environment, surrounded by people with job titles and roles that are unfamiliar to you and it seems like everyone is watching and judging your performance. The first thing to remember, when you feel like this, is that you are not alone. Most people get nervous when they start doing something new. The feeling does diminish as you become more experienced, but awkwardness in a nervous presenter will prevent the building of a rapport with the audience, who will therefore be less likely to continue watching.

Empathy

The reason why gestures such as a yawn and a burst of laughter are infectious is because human beings have an in-built ability to empathize with their fellow humans. This capacity to feel what others feel is one of the key factors that set humans apart from other beings, and is reflected in the way we 'mirror' emotions. When someone smiles at us, we invariably smile back, so long as their smile is perceived to be genuine. The ability to harmonize our feelings with the feelings of others is the way that babies and children learn. It also holds the key to survival. When one person runs, it is human nature for everyone to follow their lead.

Thankfully there are not many occasions in this day and age when we all need to run for survival, but we are all still left with the ability to empathize. Catching the eye of someone who is desperately trying not to giggle, or sitting with someone who is

The audience can sense any awkwardness in a nervous or uncertain presenter; they will be less likely to engage fully and may lose interest.

inconsolable after their pet has died, we often find ourselves laughing or crying too.

An audience will respond to genuine emotion but, if a presenter is overly nervous, there may be a sense that something is not quite right. Another issue is that anxiety may be interpreted as uncertainty. Being blissfully unaware of how intimidating a camera lens can be, let alone a TV studio, the viewer may assume that the reason a presenter appears nervous or unsure is because they do not know what they are talking about.

Warm Up

Having nerves is almost inevitable when starting out. There are, however, a few ways that you can control them. First, make sure you warm up. Do not spend the minutes leading up to filming hunched in a corner, making yourself small, with your nose in a script. If you do this, the transition between being small and quiet and big and enthusiastic will be too great and most likely a lacklustre performance will be the result. Instead, go somewhere spacious and throw your arms out wide, open yourself up and say your script out loud. Being over the top then settling your energy down

for the camera is much easier than trying to pull it up at the last minute.

Breathe

Using the 4-7-8 breathing exercise – inhale normally for four seconds, hold the breath for seven seconds and then exhale for eight seconds – can help settle your nerves before a presentation. You can also practise tongue twisters to warm up your mouth and vocal cords, and try humming to loosen your vocal folds and increase your range.

Be Prepared

One of the main reasons for being nervous (along with being new to presenting) is a lack of preparedness. The importance of being prepared comes up a lot at the TV Training Academy. Standing up in front of an audience or a camera without knowing what they are going to say is the main reason why a presenter loses confidence in their ability to present. There are times when a presenter will have to think on their feet and ad lib, but this is a very different

Sitting down quietly before presenting reduces energy levels and makes finding the performance harder. Stand up, walk around and say your script out loud before you start.

process. Indeed, ad libbing is often structured (*see* Chapter 6).

Spend as much time preparing as is humanly possible. Read through what you have to say so that there are no surprises, practise any tricky names of people or locations, fully research guests and ensure you understand agendas or key messages. It might be the case that you are employed to present on a subject that is not very familiar to you; in this case, you might wish to sign yourself up for evening classes to learn about the topic. At the very least, you should read widely around it and watch videos, so that you become completely at ease with the terminology and the processes.

Research has found that practising something for ten minutes every day for twenty-one days will greatly improve capability. Knowledge improves confidence and confidence eradicates nerves.

Visualize Success

One way of overcoming fears when you are new to presenting is to avoid focusing on what might go wrong, and to visualize the positive outcome that you are aiming for. This might be feedback from viewers, praise from the producer or the promise of future work.

Take a few moments to relax, close your eyes and imagine in great detail the feeling of presenting with complete confidence. In your mind's eye, see yourself not only doing a great job but also enjoying it. This method of visualization is used by professional and successful people all around the world and is based on psychotherapy and neuro-linguistic programming (NLP). In layman's terms, this states that the subconscious mind cannot tell the difference between what is real and what is imagined. If you picture events going well, therefore, and feel confident, your subconscious mind – which is more powerful than your conscious mind – presumes that this is just how things are and so goes about putting this state of mind into action:

What you focus on grows, what you think about expands, and what you dwell upon determines your destiny.

(Robin Sharma)

Posture

Standing up straight with good posture not only gives you authority but, according to Dr Amy Cuddy, also changes your body chemistry. Standing for two minutes or longer in what Cuddy refers to as a 'power pose' decreases cortisol and increases testosterone, providing an increased feeling of power.

A presenter with good posture will instil an air of confidence, while someone with droopy hunched shoulders will come across as weak and ineffectual. Contrary to popular belief, good posture is not simply a case of sticking the shoulders back. It is about aligning each region of the body, from the

The Wonder Woman stance – a 'power pose'. Standing with open body language for two minutes or more can make a positive difference to energy and confidence.

head down to the feet, and building core strength. There are plenty of online programmes giving advice and training on how to improve posture and there are also a number of posture support products available, such as foam rollers, resistance bands and gym balls.

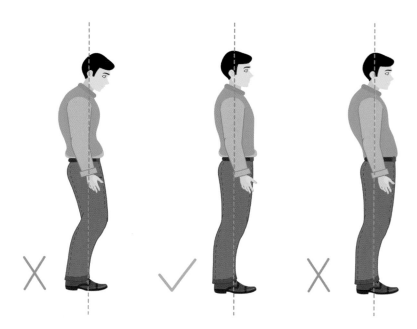

Good posture makes you look and feel more confident. It also increases energy, as the muscles are more efficient when the body is properly aligned.

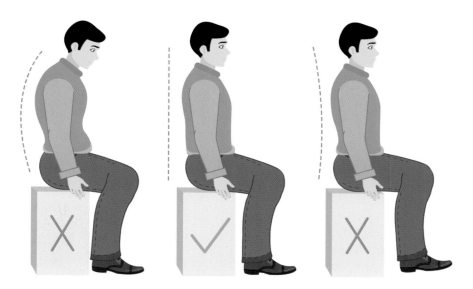

Sitting in a hunched position reduces lung capacity, which weakens vocal delivery and lowers energy levels.

DRESS THE PART

Clothes and Accessories

Apparently it takes seven seconds to form a first impression of somebody, based on what they look like, while research by Princeton University indicates that a pretty accurate assessment regarding trustworthiness is made in just one-tenth of a second. A viewer will very quickly make an assumption about a presenter based solely on their physical appearance, so good grooming and dressing appropriately are important. Neat and tidy is nearly always preferred, but sometimes it will be necessary to 'dress the part'; a children's TV show presenter, for example, will have a completely different dress code from that of a newsreader.

When choosing clothing, certain patterns are best avoided, as they may come across as too busy. For example, tight dots and tight stripes can cause a visual interference known as a moiré pattern. Full black and white clothes can cause issues too, as the contrast against skin tones can make it hard for the lighting director to get their settings correct.

It helps to know what colour the background scenery is, so that your clothes do not clash with it. This is not always possible, so it is a good idea to take an alternative outfit to change into should the need occur. Reds are usually better than greens and blues, in case you are required to stand in front of a green/blue screen.

Think about the cut of your neckline. Revealing too much cleavage or chest hair may divert attention while polo necks and scarves are too hot for studio conditions. Avoid flimsy fabrics, as these will tend to droop unfavourably if you need to have a lapel mic attached.

Jewellery that is large and obtrusive, such as dangly earrings, will be a distraction when you move your head, so keep them small and discreet. The same goes for necklaces. Metal bangles or bracelets are best avoided, particularly if you are

Tight stripes on fabric can cause an interference on screen known as a moiré pattern, also referred to as a 'zebra' pattern.

wearing more than one on the same wrist, as they will clink together or bang on a desk or podium.

It is worth checking in advance the way you are going to be shot. Most shots incorporate head and shoulders. That said, you would be wise to think about what you wear on your bottom half too just in case of last-minute changes.

Make-Up

The type of presenting you are involved in will determine whether you are expected to do your own make up or whether a make-up artist will apply it for you. It will also affect the style of your make-up and the approach that is taken. For general presenting, there are a number of useful guidelines that will help you to be prepared for most eventualities:

- The best look, especially for men, is the 'no make-up' look, which means that make-up has been applied, but in such a way as to achieve a natural and fresh-looking result.
- TV studio lights are hot, so expect to shine profusely even if this is something that does not trouble you in everyday life. A shiny face on camera is not a good look so keep powder with you at all times to apply in between takes. A balding head should be treated in the same way as the face, as it will reflect ceiling lights.
- Cameras and lights tend to wash out natural skin colour, giving you a ghostly appearance. Warmer, more neutral make-up colours can be used to accentuate natural tones.
- Make sure you apply make-up evenly, covering any blemishes, and be particularly careful to blend in foundation to avoid obvious lines.
- Do not apply more make-up than you need.
- If you are unfamiliar with applying make-up, consider taking a class. At the very least, you should visit a make-up counter in a department store and ask them to make you up and explain the process. This is often free of charge, but you may be expected to buy a selection of any products they use.

With high-definition TV (HD) becoming the norm and the prevalence of 4K and even 8K, there is a need to be even more aware of your physical appearance – the high resolution of the picture means that there is nowhere to hide. HD make-up is now widely available in most stores, offering superior light reflection, and blurring even the tiniest of lines and wrinkles. HD powder can prevent the 'cakey' clogging that can be a problem with some make-up powders. Brands offering HD ranges of powders, concealers and foundations included Mac, Make Up for Ever and Clinique.

Grooming

Another aspect of your appearance to think about is your hands, which you will be using for communication as well as for holding props and greeting people. Even if they are simply folded in front of your body, their condition will be noticeable. Make sure your nails are clean and manicured and that any rings are in keeping with the style of the show.

The camera picks up everything, and viewers can be very critical, especially when you are looming large in their sitting room. Men should pay extra attention to ensure that there are no protruding nasal hairs or overly bushy eyebrows. Similarly, discoloured or stained teeth are easily seen on a 50-inch television screen; many presenters have had theirs whitened in recent years, and you may wish to consider this, if you feel it would give you more confidence.

HELEN SHEPPARD: DIRECTOR'S SUMMARY

Being yourself might sound like the easiest thing but, when faced with a camera and a studio full of unfamiliar people, it can be a daunting experience. Having confidence in who you are, preparing well and learning the techniques will help. Make sure you are comfortable with what you are wearing, remember to smile and do not worry about being perfect!

PERFORMANCE AT A GLANCE

- Be yourself.
- Do not try too hard and avoid endlessly seeking approval.
- Don't fake it.
- Subtly increase your energy, enthusiasm and expressions, and empathize.
- Add a smile to your voice.
- Warm up, be prepared, control your breathing and with a little practice your confidence will shine.
- The best presenters don't 'present'.

3
TV AND VIDEO PRESENTING TECHNIQUES

It is all very well being able to communicate effectively but, when talking to camera, if you happen to be looking in the wrong direction or standing in the wrong place you will not be very effective as an on-screen presenter.

There are five golden rules or techniques for television and video presenting, which will ensure that your effective three-dimensional communication fits the screen and engages the audience. However, it is worth pointing out that it does not really matter if you find yourself breaking a rule once in a while. Like many rules, they are there to be broken. In fact, professional presenters do this all the time, but it must be a conscious decision on their part. It could be that the style of the show calls for a slightly different approach or maybe the presenter has decided to create some humour or make a particular point. Problems only occur when the rules are broken continuously and the presenter is not aware it is happening.

Whether you choose to incorporate these 'rules' wholly into your presenting or only aspects of them at certain times, knowing the rules and practising the techniques will provide you with a solid foundation on which to build your own personal style.

GOLDEN RULE ONE: MOVEMENT

Hands

Everybody moves when they speak and generally it is the hands that do most of the work. Using the hands is such a natural action for human beings that much of the movement happens unconsciously. When in front of a camera, however, we can suddenly become very aware of our hands and this often causes us to stop using them completely.

Our hand gestures are an extension of our speech. They help us communicate more effectively and they also aid us in composing our messages. Trying to remember a word that is on the tip of our tongue often requires us to use our hands as a prompt. According to body language expert Dr Carol Kinsey Goman, the reason we use our hands is to power up our thinking: 'Gesturing can help people form clearer thoughts, speak in tighter sentences and use more declarative language.' However, a presenter may be reading off a teleprompter, remembering a script or reciting well-prepared key notes. The conditions are not the same and do not inspire the normal, natural set of hand movements that might be created when speaking off the cuff.

'What do I do with my hands?' is one of the most common questions that new presenters ask when first standing in front of the camera. The answer to this is to do what you normally do with your hands. Imagine being in a coffee shop talking with a friend or associate. Do the same with your hands when you are presenting as you would in that setting.

The hands are used to emphasize certain words, highlight important points, show an emotion or help describe something. If we do not use our hands, the instinct to move finds a way out somewhere else. This could result in shifting

Hands in this position are ready to make a small or large gesture as and when it feels appropriate. If the fingers are interlocked or the hands are down by the side of the body, it is more of an effort to move and gestures will become very deliberate.

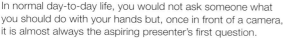

In normal day-to-day life, you would not ask someone what you should do with your hands but, once in front of a camera, it is almost always the aspiring presenter's first question.

weight from one leg to the other, rocking back and forth, flapping our arms or simply fidgeting. An accomplished presenter will use their hands just enough to control any other movements so that they do not distract from their words. This measured form of hand control instils in the viewer a sense of security. The presenter is essentially saying, 'I know what I am doing, so all you need to do is simply sit back, relax and listen.' A new presenter starting out will need to make a conscious effort to use small hand movements in order to become accustomed to the feeling. However, it is vital not to repeat the same gesture over and over again. The audience will notice a pattern very quickly and, if the movement has no correlation with what is being said, it will become distracting.

It may be helpful, when working with scripts, to think in advance about various hand movements that match the sentiment of the words. What gesture would suit a particular point or help in describing something?

Hands at rest need to be positioned in such a way that they do not draw attention away from the words

THE POWER OF HANDS

Used correctly, the hands are a great asset when presenting. Author and body language expert Vanessa Van Edwards has undertaken a study of thousands of TED talks (influential video presentations by expert speakers). She found that, over the same length of time, the most popular talks had an average of 7.4 million views and 465 hand gestures, while the least popular had an average of 124,000 views and used an average of 272 hand gestures. Van Edwards puts this down to charisma and authenticity but also, and more importantly, to the fact that the viewer has an easier time trusting someone if they can see their hands.

When the hands behave unnaturally, or remain out of sight, the viewer can be unnerved because they cannot relate to any gestures or see what the hands are doing. According to Van Edwards, the 'hidden hand syndrome' produces in humans a deeply embedded fear that stems from our cave-dwelling days, when it was expected that a person who was not showing their hands was concealing a weapon.

being spoken, whilst at the same time being ready to spring into action when needed. A standard resting position is generally waist high, palms towards the body, slightly facing up, with one hand cupped inside the other, and thumbs touching.

Body Language

In order for the hands to work on our behalf, the message they are putting out has to work in accordance with the message that is being imparted verbally. This is because our hands often act as our subconscious, and we cannot control that aspect of our behaviour. If somebody says the word 'BIG', but their hands indicate 'small', the highly attuned viewer, whether they realize it or not, will subconsciously pick up on the discrepancy. We are, after all, not very far evolved from our ancestors, who were speaking through their bodies long before the development of verbal communication. In the animal world, body language can mean the difference between life and death, which is why human beings often know what the body is saying without realizing it.

Consciously reading body language is a very complex business. One signal used in isolation could have a variety of different meanings. When a body language expert is analysing a subject, they look for a group of signals known as a cluster. These signals may take the form of speech patterns and tonality, eye movements, facial expressions and body movements. Only when several signals are suggesting the same meaning can an expert make an informed assessment.

Crossed arms give the impression that the person is being defensive.

Hands on hips with the thumbs facing back could indicate readiness and enthusiasm to start something.

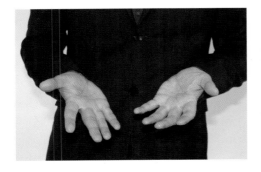

Palms up are often thought of as a sign of trust; you are not concealing anything and have nothing to hide.

Hands clenched with the fingers interlocked often signifies frustration, anxiety or holding back.

'Steepling' fingers can be a sign of control, power or authority.

Clasping hands and rubbing fingers is a self-pacifying gesture and can indicate an uncomfortable feeling – usually nerves or fear.

Clasping hands tightly with no movement can show stress and anxiety.

There are some body positions that may imply certain meanings over others, so it is important for a presenter to be aware of these and how they may be interpreted.

Movement is also directly connected to confidence. A confident presenter, comfortable with the message they are conveying, will move in a different way from a presenter who is ill at ease or defensive. A presenter who is uncomfortable may use their body, and especially the hands, as a metaphorical shield to protect them from the words they are saying. Such a pose immediately creates a barrier between the presenter's words and the way they are being interpreted by the viewer.

When thoughts and hands become disconnected, the brain slows down, and you may find yourself fumbling for words. If this happens, take a pause and return your hands to the rest position. This should restore your confidence and enable you to re-engage the brain and get everything back on track.

The type of show being presented will determine whether you are standing, sitting, lying on a bed, bouncing on a bungee cord or moving around. In each scenario, different rules of body language (if any) will apply. There are, however, some basic techniques, which are relevant in the majority of situations.

STANDING

If a presenter is standing to attention, front on to the camera, it can sometimes look a little too formal or even aggressive. To relax this, stand instead with one foot slightly forward, hips angled at around 30 degrees to the camera, shoulders down and hands in the rest position ready to go.

In order to look confident and relaxed, you need to keep your feet anchored to the floor and your legs still. Let the top half of your body and hands do the moving. Even the slightest lower-half wobble – the sway of a leg or the bounce of a toe – if it is continuous, can indicate nerves, which the viewer will detect. Left unchecked, small

Standing face on to the camera can look very formal, reminiscent of a military person standing to attention.

Putting one foot slightly forward and having the hands in the rest position has a relaxed feel and is a good place from which to start.

movements can develop into larger ones – shifting weight from one leg to the other or taking a step forward and back, for example. Clearly, this can be an issue when working on camera, especially with a close-up shot, as the presenter might move partially or even fully out of the picture.

When you are presenting in a studio in a standing position, you will usually be given a place to put yourself, which will be marked on the studio floor with gaffer tape in the form of a T. It is important to be in the right spot as this is likely to be a camera focus point or the location where a microphone has been set. The centre 'leg' of the T should be right in the middle of where you are standing and your toes should just touch its crossbar.

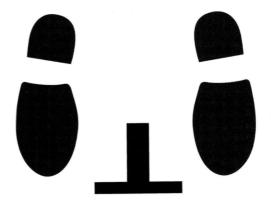

A mark on the floor in the form of a T is used to indicate where the presenter should stand.

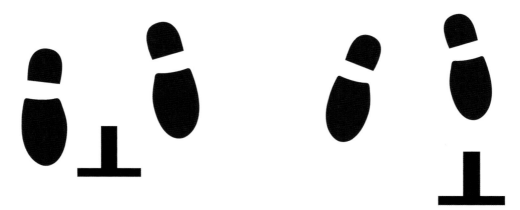

'Hitting the mark' requires the presenters' toes to be close to the crossbar of the T.

An incorrect position: off-centre and too far away from the mark.

It is not always the case that a presenter has to stay pinned in one place. On location, for example, you may be required to present to camera whilst walking and, in a studio, you may need to move in order to demonstrate something. When moving to a new marked position, you will need to be able to judge the position of the T without looking directly down at the floor. This is known as 'hitting your mark'.

If presenting to a live audience, good stagecraft requires an element of movement, allowing you to engage with all sides by occasionally walking to a new spot. When you move, make sure you do it

Constantly meandering around a stage is known as 'travelling' and can make a presenter look uneasy. When you move, do so with purpose and then stand still until you make the decision to move again.

with purpose; avoid meandering or aimless wandering, and try not to get side-tracked halfway. Equally, on arrival at the fixed location, stop and anchor yourself so that you are still from the waist down. This indicates that you are assertive and sure of yourself.

SITTING

Presenters are very often expected to present sitting down. The same rules apply as for standing: keep the lower half of the body anchored, so that any movement comes from your upper half only. Try to avoid slouching or leaning too heavily to one side or the other, as this can look too relaxed or even sloppy. To give a more professional impression, sit upright with a straight back; it helps if you have your bottom at the back of the chair. Once in this position try to keep your lower half still. You can turn to face whoever may be talking, but you need to avoid fidgeting.

Having your legs crossed is often a good idea, but you need to be aware that a number of different camera angles may be used in the studio. If your knees are just slightly too far apart, you may be the victim of an unflattering shot!

Crossing your legs at the ankles or the knees is usually acceptable, but crossing your legs with one ankle on the other knee can appear too relaxed or again find an unflattering camera angle.

Sitting with crossed ankles or knees together is usually a safe bet when working in a multi-camera studio.

Some seated positions can be unflattering, depending on the camera angle. Presenters need to be particularly careful when sitting on a low sofa.

Movement at a Glance

- Keep your feet anchored to the ground and your upper half relaxed.
- Use your hands to work in conjunction with what you have to say.
- Move with purpose.
- Be aware of and avoid continuous or repetitive movements.

GOLDEN RULE TWO: EYE CONTACT

When a presenter looks into the lens of a camera, the viewer feels that this person is looking into their eyes and speaking directly to them. This, of course, is not the presenter's experience when looking into the camera lens, as it is an inanimate metal object. However, the illusion for the viewer is a powerful one, which makes them feel engaged and an important part of the proceedings.

While we interpret body language to gauge a person's overall state of mind, we zone in on the eyes to work out the more precise details. The reason eye contact is so important is because it allows us to evaluate the intentions and authenticity of others. If we suspect someone of lying, we focus our attention on their eyes.

If it is true that 'the eyes are the window to the soul', then eye contact with another person causes great quantities of data to pass back and forth; this happens both consciously and subconsciously, and relates to love, hate, intelligence, sincerity, strength, weakness, happiness and sadness. If the contact is broken in an unnatural manner, so

Looking directly into the camera lens gives the audience at home the impression that you are speaking to them, and involving them in the activities taking place in the studio.

PART OF THE PACK

Pack animals will look to their leader's reaction to an event to ascertain whether the group should run, attack or stand their ground. It is an important instinct, as working together gives the group and the individuals a far greater chance of survival. Human beings have similar traits, left over from our ancestors. We have an inherent desire to be accepted by the group, to fit in and not be left behind.

That there is any kind of social hierarchy within a group of friends may not be obvious but there is a simple way of identifying who might be 'top dog'. When there is a group conversation, look at who it is that the majority of the group glance at when something provokes a reaction. That is top dog.

Good eye contact makes us feel that we are part of the group, that we are included and that we will not be left behind. This concept is also relevant in multi-camera presenting (see Chapter 4) and a technique called an 'aside'.

too is the trust in what is being said. This does not happen instantly with one stray glance, but it will be noticed if it happens repeatedly. Most commonly, eye contact is broken when one of the communicators feels out of sorts, exposed, self-conscious or intimidated. Conversely, the ability to maintain good eye contact for the full duration of a conversation shows strength of character, confidence, power, sincerity and/or honesty.

Maintaining eye contact is not as straightforward as simply staring into the eyes of another person. A study conducted by the Science Museum to establish preferred length of eye contact found that, on average, humans can cope with three seconds of uninterrupted eye contact if in a group and up to nine seconds if one-on-one. Any longer, and discomfort creeps in, creating a sense of unease and intimidation. This, however, does not apply when the eye contact comes via the screen. The viewer is aware that they cannot be seen by the person on the screen, and this means that they are comfortable with the eye contact being constant.

It is also worth noting that we read people's eyes whether they are in contact with our own eyes or not. When watching an interview or interaction, we will judge responses and comments through the eyes of the people involved. For example, if the eyes of the person who is speaking are darting quickly between two listeners, it suggests

insecurity, as they seem to be desperately looking for a response or reassurance.

Eyes on the Lens

One of the hardest aspects of television or video presenting is getting used to talking into the lens and receiving no form of feedback. When we speak face to face with another person, numerous messages are passed via facial expressions and eye contact, by both the speaker and the receiver. When we are engaged in conversation, we look for a response to what we are saying – it might be reassurance, humour, concern, interest or even boredom. It is all very subtle, but it is instinctively understood and responded to accordingly.

When we are communicating via a lens, none of these cues exist. The presenter has no idea how their words are being interpreted, and this can be disconcerting. Sometimes, a new presenter is so confused by this that they look away from the lens in order to seek out a human face that can offer them the response they crave. In doing so, they instantly break the connection with the viewer at home. Looking into a lens while talking feels unnatural, so there is always a temptation to look away, whether there are other people close by or not. Breaking eye contact with the lens can give the presenter a micro-moment of relief from an uncomfortable

If a presenter keeps looking off the lens, it can give the impression that something is going on to the side, and the audience is not being told about it. It can also make the presenter look nervous and unsure of themselves.

situation. The same can be achieved with rapid and continuous blinking, but it also can make the presenter look a little insecure and unsure.

A quick glance away from the lens from time to time is unlikely to bother the audience, or even be noticed by them, but repeatedly looking off lens or continuously seeking a reaction from a member of the crew can give an impression of untrustworthiness. The viewer has no idea why the presenter is looking away, or what they are looking at, so their feeling of being included and involved is momentarily spoilt.

Good eye contact with the lens allows the audience to focus on what is being said without constantly wondering what might be happening off screen.

If you have ever spoken to someone who cannot look at you in the eye when talking to you, you will know the feeling. Being able to keep good eye contact with the lens is essential, but it is also important to know when you can and even should look away.

Eyes off the Lens

Of course, there are many instances when a presenter will be right to take their eyes off the lens; for example, it would be strange if a presenter was talking to a guest and did not look at them at all. The rule is that, if the audience can see someone or something, or they know that it is there, the presenter can look at it too. So, looking at the guest during an interview is perfectly normal, as is looking at anything in shot that is being spoken about. If the audience can see what the presenter is looking at, there is no risk of them feeling excluded.

The presenter can also look off lens as long as they mention what it is that they are looking at. This way, the audience are being kept in the picture and again any feeling of exclusion is avoided.

Another instance where losing contact with the lens is acceptable is when looking away in order to think. As the average person is so adept at reading facial expressions, they will understand and accept what is happening if occasionally a presenter averts their eyes from the lens in contemplation.

Live on Stage

When it comes to addressing a live audience, none of the above applies because the situation is similar to a face-to-face conversation. The audience will not object to the presenter's eyes being elsewhere, because they will be aware that there are other people in the room. If they wish, they may even turn around in their seats to look at whatever it is that has caught the presenter's eye. They are able to see everything that the presenter can see.

When it comes to eye contact, one technique for engaging with a live audience is to look at an individual audience member, hold the gaze for two or three seconds, then move on to do the same to someone else. This random eye contact can be continued for the full length of the presentation.

If the audience knows what the presenter is looking at, or can see it, there is no issue with breaking eye contact with the lens.

The audience can see the difference between a presenter glancing off camera due to nerves or genuinely reflecting on what to say next.

Eye Contact at a Glance

- Keep your eyes on the lens unless the viewer can see or knows what you are looking at.
- Do not be tempted to look for a reaction from people behind the camera or elsewhere in the studio.
- Be mindful of using calm and considered eye movements and avoid rapid blinking or flicks.

GOLDEN RULE THREE: TALK TO ONE PERSON

More often than not, people watch television and online videos on their own or in small gatherings of no more than two or three. Rarely is there an audience in the usual sense of the word, unless it is a sporting or other major event. The experience of the person watching, then, is more akin to having a chat in a coffee shop than to attending a speech. A presenter who starts a video or TV show with the words 'Hello, Ladies and Gentlemen' immediately destroys any sense that the viewer might just be meeting up with a friend.

Starting from the premise that there is a live audience watching will change the way you speak to the camera. When public speaking, people generally use bigger movements and gestures, and a louder voice, and are more formal. If you talked to someone like that in their living room, it would be over the top and uncomfortable for them, to say the least. For a presenter, the thought that they are speaking to potentially hundreds of thousands of people is also likely to cause a sharp increase in nerves and anxiety, which will have an effect on the way they speak. It is far better for both presenter and audience if the presenter imagines that the camera is their best friend, and engages in a natural and chatty way.

Talk to a Friend

Remember, 'the best presenters do not present'. Instead, they use their imagination or memory to create the 'mood' that is needed for on-screen presenting. One technique that can help achieve this is to think of a friend – real or imaginary – with whom you feel totally comfortable. Create a picture of them in your mind's eye and, every time the camera rolls, imagine you are just chatting to them as easily and naturally as you would if you were sitting opposite one another. Some presenters even place a photo of their 'friend' just below the lens. You might find this is something that helps you.

Talk to the camera in the same way you would chat with a friend in a coffee shop.

Staring at the lens for any length of time will make your eyes glaze over and become vacant-looking.

Seeing reactions in your mind's eye or imagining a friend's face can trick you into talking to the camera in a natural way.

There is no need to stop at simply picking a friend and imagining you are chatting to them. You can also conjure up the best possible reactions and responses they will give to what you are saying. Identify the way you impart humour that seems to make your friend laugh, or ways in which you could get them looking interested in what you have to say. Give yourself the best responses; remember, your subconscious cannot tell the difference between the real world and something that has been created by your imagination, so feed it positivity.

The more you are able to convince yourself that you are engaging with a friend, the easier presenting to camera becomes and the more convincing it is for the viewer to watch. One extra benefit of using this approach is that the rule about keeping 'eyes on the lens' becomes even more effective. It is very easy for your eyes to seem to glaze over if you are just staring at a lens for any length of time. However, if you can picture your friend's face in place of the lens, reacting and responding to what you are saying, your eyes will come alive.

Live Audiences

Some TV shows will have a live audience as well as an audience at home. In this instance, it is perfectly acceptable to greet the room with a 'Good Evening, Ladies and Gentlemen', because this is a less intimate setting, and there are indeed ladies and gentlemen there who can be seen by the audience at home. Just because you are presenting to a live audience, however, does not mean you have to up the formality. Remain as informal as you would be if you were talking one-on-one; this way, you remain fully relatable.

When presenting to camera, the illusion that you are creating is that it is just you, the presenter, talking to an individual viewer. If the viewer were to think about it, they would of course be aware that you are talking not just to them but to thousands of people. It is your job as a presenter, in that case, to ensure that they have no reason to start thinking about it.

If there is an audience in the studio, viewers at home are comfortable to assume that they are part of that group of people.

Talk to One Person at a Glance

- Find a 'friend' and talk to them.
- Keep it chatty and personable.
- Keep it one-on-one unless addressing an audience.
- Be presumptuous and imagine positive feedback coming from your 'friend'.

GOLDEN RULE FOUR: UP ON THREE

The Silent Count

When you are presenting to camera, whether in a studio, on location, live or pre-record, the cue to start usually begins with a countdown. This could be a floor manager or member of the crew counting down on their fingers from ten. The numbers will be spoken out loud until four, and then three-two-one will be silent, using hand signals only.

The reason for the silent count is to avoid any possibility of the last part of the countdown being audible on the take or broadcast. Occasionally, a live television programme might get a late or early handover, so a three-second 'buffer' is put in place as a safety margin. The term 'Up on three' refers to the presenter being prepared and ready to go on the three of the countdown, in case of an early handover. It is also normal for filming that is not live (a pre-record) to begin in the same way, as it gives the editor a clean start during post-production.

The presenter must have their eyes on the lens and be ready with good energy on three. If they are looking at the floor manager's hand signals and wait until the very last moment to look at the camera, the audience may catch their eyes still

A countdown to the start of a show or take is usually signalled from ten with hand signals and a verbal call. Up to four there will be both a verbal call and a hand signal.

From three in the countdown, there will be a hand signal only, with the verbal call stopping. This will ensure a clean start to the audio.

At two in the countdown, there will be a hand signal only.

The one count is also a hand signal only and is followed by the cue for the presenter to start. This is normally a pointing gesture.

If the presenter waits until the cue to start before looking at the lens and bringing some warmth to their face, the sudden jump into action may be caught by the viewer.

To avoid an obvious transition, the presenter should have their eyes on the lens, warmth in the eyes and be ready, or 'up', from the three count.

moving to the lens – even if the handover is perfectly timed. Similarly, if the presenter is waiting until the last moment to smile, and find the 'you on a good day' mood, the transition is obvious and they will look fake right from the start.

To avoid any chance of the viewer catching the transition, your eyes should be on the lens and you should be in the correct mood on the three count. It is generally a good idea to have some warmth in your face at that moment too, especially if you are welcoming the viewer to the show or video.

At the end of a live show, another countdown with hand signals will give the presenter a clear indication of when the programme is about to finish. Depending on the type of show being produced, the presenter may turn to any guests and thank them, look down at papers on the desk and shuffle them, or just smile at the camera. Whichever finishing scenario is being used, the presenter must maintain the 'performance' until a 'cut' is called by the director or producer.

The same applies to a pre-record: the presenter should hold the last thought (usually warmth) while saying goodbye and be careful to keep eye contact with the lens, as this will give the editor some scope to add fades or effects into the titles. If the presenter immediately drops the 'performance' and looks off lens, the editor has little room for creativity.

During any countdown the floor manager will be as close to the camera as possible, to allow the presenter to use their peripheral vision to follow the hand signals. On a live or 'as live' show, the presenter may also have an earpiece (talkback), so that they can hear the countdowns and have no need to look out for the hand signals.

Up on 3 at a Glance

- Be ready on the three count.
- Wait until 'cut' is called before finishing.
- Use your peripheral vision to see hand signals.

GOLDEN RULE FIVE: HANDLING MISTAKES

Communication is not an exact science. Everyone stutters a little from time to time, says the wrong thing or trips over a word, but generally it is barely noticeable, and only referenced – usually with humour – when it is a really obvious fluff. Put someone in front of a camera, however, and they inevitably want to be perfect. However, the ability to take any imperfections in their stride makes a presenter more relatable and human – remember the example of the actress making smoothies!

Making a Blunder

A presenter can be their own worst critic, putting themselves under the microscope and noticing every single imperfection – many of which, incidentally, will not be spotted by the audience. In these cases, it is good discipline simply to carry on in the same way as you would in a real-life conversation. That is what is expected of a professional presenter.

On live television or streaming, there is no stopping and trying again. Imagine having a conversation over coffee with a friend, when she forgets someone's name. She does not say, 'Sorry, can I start that again?' If she did, it would be quite bizarre.

Often, it is not the mistake that is the problem, but the way it is handled once it has been made. If, for example, you stop mid-sentence, or apologize when you have mispronounced or stumbled on a word, it is much more noticeable than simply carrying on and letting the mistake pass.

If the mistake is obvious, the best way to cope with it is simply to smile. If it fits your personality,

Looking annoyed or apologizing for a minor stutter or mispronunciation simply draws attention to it. Carry on without a care and generally the audience will not even notice it.

If you are embarrassed or uncomfortable with your mistakes, the audience will feel embarrassed or uncomfortable for you.

you could say something like 'I'll just put my false teeth in and try that again'. This instantly reassures the viewer that you are human and there is nothing to worry about. Mistakes happen, and the audience will be fully able to empathize.

SMILE

When someone smiles, they are creating a symbiotic relationship with the person they are smiling at, releasing feel-good endorphins in the brain of both. As a consequence, both enjoy a feeling of reward. What is more, the contagion does not stop there. In 2019, American psychologists published the results of nearly 50 years of data and the study of 11,000 people and concluded that not only does smiling make people happier, but also scowling makes them more angry and frowning makes them more sad. If you are able to smile naturally when presenting, you will come across as someone who is relaxed, personable and comfortable in both who you are and in the message that you are imparting.

Honesty is the Best Policy

No matter how well you plan for all eventualities, sometimes things that are out of your control can and do go wrong. Unless it is a catastrophic disaster, it is unlikely the viewer will notice. However, if it is obvious, honesty is the best policy. Do not try to hide it or pretend it has not happened. If it is clear that the audience will be aware that something is amiss, bring them in on it so that they feel included. If appropriate, use humour. Your viewers will enjoy being in on the joke.

Another time when being honest can be helpful for a presenter is when you get the giggles, also known as 'corpsing'. You may be thinking that this is the least of your worries, especially if you are new to the business, but you might be surprised. There have been some studies that suggest that uncontrollable laughing is the brain's way of diffusing tension and coping with stress, both of which can be common issues in a TV studio. Sometimes, all it takes is the most unlikely trigger! The more you try to hide it, the worst it gets, so the best way to diffuse the situation is to simply tell the audience what it is that is making you laugh. This, more often than not, is all it takes.

Serious Mistakes

Sometimes, something is said on a live broadcast that has serious implications, although this is rare. Such incidents must be handled in a professional manner. The broadcast industry is regulated by the Government department known as OFCOM, which investigates any complaints that are made regarding TV, radio or on-demand content. The reasons for a complaint might range from the use of offensive language to a libellous statement, and the regulator may require the matter to be addressed by the presenter live on air. If you are asked by your producer to retract anything you have said, you need to ensure this is done formally and sincerely. After the statement, you should continue with the programme as if the event never happened.

HELEN SHEPPARD: DIRECTOR'S SUMMARY

These five golden rules are so useful. Whether standing or sitting, make sure you are comfortable. Keeping eye contact with the camera is vital; imagine you are talking to a friend and keep your delivery natural and chatty. Smiling and not worrying about mistakes will help your confidence. Relax and let your enthusiasm shine through.

Handling Mistakes at a Glance

- If you make a mistake, carry on; chances are the viewer has not even noticed.
- If you make an obvious mistake, smile and/or treat it lightheartedly if that is appropriate.
- If a serious mistake is made, follow the producer's instructions in a professional manner.
- If fluffing or tripping over the odd word does not bother you, it will not bother the audience either.
- Be honest with the viewer and they will trust you.

4
TOOLS OF THE TRADE

Technical skill is mastery of complexity, while creativity is mastery of simplicity.

(Erik Christopher Zeeman)

While confidence, charisma and the ability to engage with an audience are vital aspects of presenting, so too is the ability to use the equipment in every production studio. As a presenter, particularly working on television, you do not work in isolation. You are highly dependent on a crew for ensuring the smooth running of the show. It is therefore essential that you know how to work within the expectations of the programming network, and as part of the team.

There are a number of essential tools and techniques that are used by presenters when in a studio, outdoors or live on air. It is important to note that simply knowing what the tools are and

Television programmes often have a large production crew made up of trained professionals. The presenter is just one part of a well-oiled machine.

Like any other member of the crew, the presenter needs to understand and be able to use any of the equipment they are given to do their job.

theoretically how they work is not enough. You also need to try them out. Never has the old adage of 'practice makes perfect' been more fitting, but do make sure you are practising in the correct way. You do not want to put hours of practice into doing something wrong.

Ideally, by the time you are ready to launch your presenting career, you will be fully familiar with the tools and techniques to the point that working with them comes across as second nature.

MULTI-CAMERA PRESENTING

Live TV shows have numerous cameras on the studio floor, all assigned to capturing different angles, aspects and elements of the show. A large-scale production may have eight cameras or more, each of which is sending an output to the show's control room. Known as the gallery, this is where the sound and vision mixer, audio engineers and producer/director are located. It is their job to look at all the footage coming from the studio and to choose the best of it for broadcast.

When presenting in a multi-camera studio it is important to maintain the sense that you are talking to just one or two people. Do not get caught up in the excitement of it all. Remember, your job is to keep the audience engaged and one effective way of achieving this is with an 'aside'. This is when a presenter has a quick look to camera after something has been said that may provoke a reaction in the viewer. In a group of friends, people tend to look

BE ADAPTABLE

Working as part of a team means that you need to know how to listen to advice, take on new ideas and, if necessary, take risks. Being professional is knowing how to conduct yourself when sometimes other people's views might be out of keeping with your own.

Every producer and director has their own way of working and, until you either own the production company or the name of the show is yours, you have to fit in, not be difficult and definitely not be a diva. Producers want to know that, when they employ you to do a job, you can be relied upon 100 per cent to do it well in all aspects.

The gallery is the behind-the-scenes control room of a TV studio.

around to see how others are reacting to what has been said (see Chapter 3), and this is the reason for an aside. Of course, if you glance at the camera lens, you will not see any reaction, but it is another way of giving a feeling of inclusion to the viewer. You can also add in an expression to the camera, maybe a quizzical look, if something does not quite make sense, or a look of surprise if it is unexpected. The key to a good aside is timing. Simply turning to the camera randomly and smiling will not look genuine.

You may also be required to change from one camera to another as you are speaking, possibly during an intro or outro. This makes for a more interesting visual dynamic to the show, but the viewer should not be aware of or distracted by these camera transitions. The movement should be smooth and natural without any pauses. Imagine that you are talking with two friends – as you speak, you look from one friend to the other, all in one flowing movement.

Each camera in a studio normally has a tally light, which indicates when it is live. The red tally light can be easily seen without needing to look directly at it.

If there are numerous cameras in operation, you will know which one is live because it will have a cue or tally light lit up. The tally light is usually red, so it can be easily seen in the presenter's peripheral vision. You may also hear the producer in the gallery calling the camera shots through your earpiece or talkback.

TALKBACK

Live television is arguably the most exciting experience for a TV presenter. It is all about acting on your wits, trusting your crew, and being prepared for all eventualities. When you are live on air, there are no take twos. As long as you are confident about all aspects of your job, it is impossible not to be swept up in the high adrenalin and immediacy of the moment. Anything can happen on live TV and, as the face of the show, it is your ability to react to the unexpected and adapt to quick-fire changes that will make or break the end result.

When presenting live, the most important tool – and in all probability the one that takes the most getting used to – is the talkback system.

Talkback is the way your producer will communicate with you when you are positioned in front of the camera. It consists of a small earpiece that is attached to a receiver pack via a transparent tube and through it you receive verbal messages and instructions from the gallery. The gallery also communicates with the crew on the studio floor, so camera operators, runners and floor managers all have talkback, enabling the producer or director to control the show. It is via talkback that you may be informed of time checks, upcoming advert breaks, news items, camera positions, and unforeseen problems. The skill in using the system lies in your being able to take on board verbal instructions at the same time as presenting, as the producer may be speaking to you (or indeed any other member of the crew) through the earpiece while you are on air.

The talkback equipment used by members of the crew is very different from the presenter's. As the crew are not in vision there is no need for a discreet earpiece and transparent tube, so usually they will have a large set of headphones, often referred to as 'cans'. The cans have a small microphone attached to enable them to talk back to the gallery.

During a live broadcast a presenter receives instructions, time counts and any essential information from the director through the earpiece, or talkback.

The crew working on the studio floor communicate with the gallery via a headset and mic, a device that is often referred to as 'cans'.

earpiece acts more like a walkie-talkie. If the producer wishes to speak to the presenter, they push a switch that opens the channel; when it is released, the channel is closed. When they are not speaking directly to the presenter, the earpiece is silent. Although closed talkback is less distracting for the presenter, it does run the risk of making them feel isolated from everything going on around them. In the vast majority of studios, there is a choice of open or closed talkback.

Practising and Auditioning with Talkback

You can practise the skills of talkback using a hands-free earpiece and your mobile phone. Ask a friend to call you on the phone and either read out a page of a book to you, or give you time counts and instruction, while you are pretending to present to camera.

Learning to talk, listen and filter out all extraneous chatter, all at the same time, is an essential aspect of live presenting. This is why it is important to be fully comfortable with the process prior to embarking on any screen tests or auditions. It

Open Talkback

In open talkback, all channels between you and the rest of the crew are left open so that, if necessary, you can be party to the many different conversations taking place within the studio. The benefit is that the presenter knows exactly what is going on around them at all times, and it is the preferred method for many experienced presenters, as it keeps them in the loop and removes any element of surprise. It takes a fair amount of practice to work with open talkback, however, as you need to become proficient at distinguishing which communication is relevant and which you can safely block out.

Closed Talkback

The other option is closed talkback, sometimes referred to as switch talkback. This is when the

EARPIECES

When auditioning for a live show, you will probably be handed a generic earpiece to use. This earpiece might fit your ear, but it is quite likely to be either too big or too small, to get stuck in your ear or keep falling out. Whatever the scenario, it will be distracting. An experienced presenter will have their own earpiece, which will have been moulded specifically to their ear size and shape and so will fit perfectly. If you are intending to audition regularly, you would be well advised to acquire a pair of your own. A simple online search will bring up plenty of companies offering the service. The advice is usually to have one for each ear, so that you can wear either left or right, depending on which side is off camera.

is not an uncommon sight to see new presenters in auditions stopping whatever they are saying mid-flow, as they are distracted by a voice in their ear. The audience should not be aware that there is someone else communicating with the presenter, as it breaks the illusion of the one-to-one conversation. That said, it is not unknown for a presenter to break this rule, it might be the case that a presenter points out that they are getting instructions from the gallery or producer for entertainment value or to keep the audience involved in what is happening.

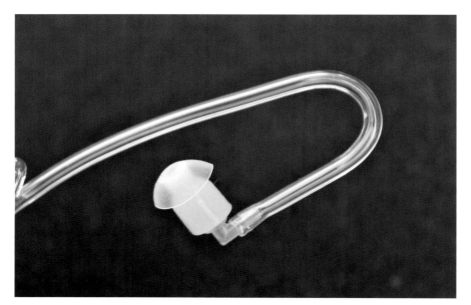

A generic earpiece – a one-size-fits-all talkback solution – can cause extra stress if it is a bad fit and is constantly falling out.

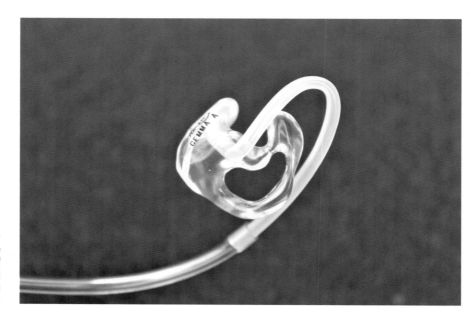

Most professional presenters have an earpiece moulded to the shape of their ear, making an exact fit and ensuring that it stays in properly.

WORKING TO TIME

With Live TV, timing is everything. Every minute of the show is accounted for and has to fit into a complex jigsaw puzzle consisting of advert breaks, credits, interviews, pre-recorded segments and day-long television schedules. On pre-recorded shows, it is possible to play with time in post-production. Editors can cut segments, add music and insert extra shots. Presenters can also re-do intros and outros and full retakes. When it comes to live TV, however, the timing has to be precise the first time around.

Working to time goes hand in hand with talk-back, as the majority of communication you receive through your earpiece will be timing related. When presenting live, your job is to engage and entertain, not to be looking at the clock, counting the seconds until the next ad break. That is the job of the director sitting in the gallery, who is there to inform the presenter of all upcoming transitions. As the end of your segment approaches, the director will start counting down:

> 10 seconds to adverts. 9-8-7-6-5-4-3-2-1-cut and clear.

Alternatively, if you are presenting, for example, a three-minute interview after which the show moves on to a cooking section (also known as an item), you will hear the director saying something like:

> One minute in.
> Two minutes gone one remaining.
> 30 seconds, standing by camera four [or whichever camera is on the kitchen set].
> 15 seconds.
> 10-9-8-7-6-5-4-3-2-1- and cue camera four.

The presenter must make sure they finish speaking just before the 'one' and not after.

It is important to know that the times at which adverts air is set in stone. Regardless of whether you have finished speaking or not, the show will cut to the ads, but you will never be 'surprised' by an ad break as you will always receive several seconds' warning from the gallery. It is most important to avoid a sloppy ending; being interrupted mid-sentence comes across as highly unprofessional. As soon as you hear the countdown you need to be prepared to deliver either a suitable close to the show (an outro) or a link to the next item on the programme.

Usually, these types of show use teleprompter links and outros, as they can be easily timed. As a rule of thumb, teleprompter text is written at three words per second for short pieces to camera (PTCs) and 150 words per minute for longer scripts. Although teleprompters are widely used for live television, this is not always the case. For some types of programme and online video, the presenter is expected to round up with no script at all. For more on structuring intros and outros, *see* Chapter 6.

USING A TELEPROMPTER OR AUTOCUE

Often used by a presenter to help them read their script, a teleprompter is a piece of electronic equipment that attaches to a video camera and

The teleprompter allows a presenter to read a script while keeping their eye line very close to the camera lens.

displays the text. It is commonly known as an Autocue, in reference to the trading name of the leading provider. The advantage of the Autocue is that it enables the presenter to maintain eye contact with the audience while appearing to speak off the top of their head.

With an Autocue, the script is displayed on a monitor sitting beneath an angled screen that reflects the text. Lying behind the reflective screen is a camera. As you read the script, you are, essentially, looking straight into the camera lens. On the left-hand side of the Autocue there is a marker indicating the line where your eyes will be making direct eye contact with the lens. This is known as the sweet spot and is the line you need to aim for.

AUTOCUE

Autocue is the brand name of the first and probably most successful of all teleprompters. It was invented, patented and licensed in the 1950s by Autocue in the UK and QTV in America. Prior to its invention, presenters were expected to memorize great swathes of information or to rely on hand-held notes. Before the mainstream use of PCs, the scripts were composed of mechanized paper scrolls, but nowadays the process is fully digitalized.

In most TV studios, the teleprompters used are Autocue/QTV Master Series 12" devices, which have brightly lit text that can be clearly read beneath the glare of the studio lights.

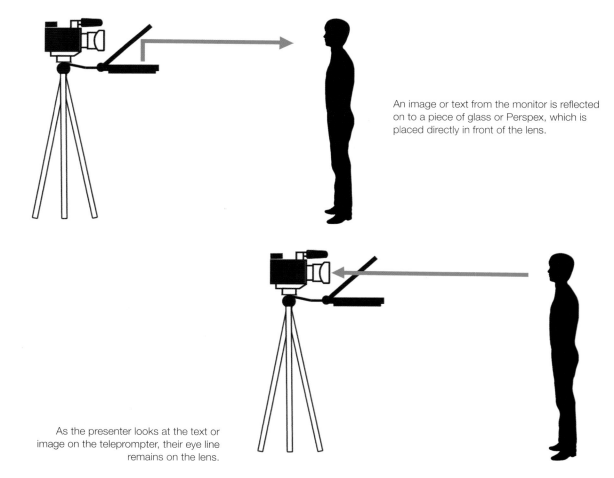

An image or text from the monitor is reflected on to a piece of glass or Perspex, which is placed directly in front of the lens.

As the presenter looks at the text or image on the teleprompter, their eye line remains on the lens.

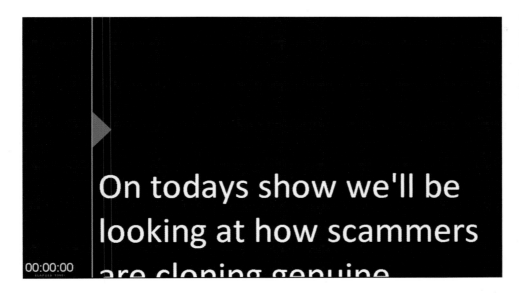

On todays show we'll be
looking at how scammers
are cloning genuine

00:00:00

The camera lens sits directly behind the line that is indicated by the marker, which is sometimes a grey triangle.

Becoming Familiar with the Script

Reading off an Autocue might seem very simple – look at the screen and read the words – but the teleprompter should be viewed only as a tool to help you. It is not a quick fix to avoid having to prepare or an opportunity to 'wing it'. As with all tools, you need to be completely familiar with how it works. The reason reading off an Autocue appears simple is because professional presenters have put in the time and effort to master the skill and to create an air of ease.

When working with an Autocue, it is not just a case of reading the words before you. Anyone can read. A presenter's role is to bring the words to life, to impart them in such a way that they come across as naturally as if you were having a face-to-face conversation. To be capable of creating this illusion you will need to be fully comfortable with the script.

It is very unlikely that you will ever be expected to read an Autocue blind on air – that is to say, without having seen the script beforehand. There may be occasions when a newsreader is required to perform this task, if there is breaking news during a live broadcast, for example, but normally a presenter will receive a hard copy in advance. It is vital that you read through this script several times and think about the meaning of the words. Make a note of what aspects of the text are important or need a different tone or feeling. If the subject matter is about tragedy or personal loss, your delivery should have a very different feel from that of a story about winning the lottery. Try to find a connection with what you will be saying. Remember, if you do not feel anything about it, the audience will not either and they might as well read the script for themselves.

Learn how to pronounce the names of people or places correctly and, if there is a word that you are not familiar with, ask the producer what it means or how it is pronounced. It is far better to ask a question off air than to be caught out on air. Write them out phonetically if it helps and practise them so that they flow. No one other than you and the Autocue operator is going to see your hard copy or your electronic device, so you can prepare the text however you want. Some presenters even use emoji icons to remind them of the sentiment or feel of the paragraph.

websites to steal customers money.
☺Plus, Conservationists release 26 penguins back into the wild after they had

00:00:22

A script on Autocue will not be seen by the audience, so anything that helps the presenter hit the right tone or pronunciation can be displayed.

Delivery

Unless something obviously gives the game away, the audience will not generally be aware that the presenter is using an Autocue at all. One common mistake when reading off an Autocue is to keep your hands still. Movement tends to find a way out when we talk, and sometimes reading off an Autocue will cause you to bounce your head in time with each word as you read. This is known as 'conducting'. However small the bounces might be, if they are not accompanied by hand movements, they will stand out against an otherwise still body. This can look very strange, to say the least. To avoid conducting and other unnatural movements, you need to become accustomed to using your hands, even when they are not needed to help you formulate your thoughts and words. Small, conscious micro hand gestures usually balance out the movement and hide any conducting.

If the audience suspects that a presenter is not simply talking to them, they may become distracted and start looking too closely at what else is going on. Your job as a presenter is to ensure that the audience never gets distracted and that their focus remains on the content or subject matter.

Vocal Variety

It is very important to use punctuation when you are reading from a teleprompter. Full stops, commas and question marks all act as signposts to the text and should not be ignored. A full stop can mark a subtle change of thought, whereas a new paragraph might be more obvious. If there is a question mark, make the words sound like a question; similarly, if there is an exclamation mark, use the appropriate emphasis to highlight the point.

The key to bringing a script off the page is to vary your inflections and emphasis. Do not just rely on the punctuation to vary your delivery. Remember, trust yourself and, if it feels right, stress a word or highlight a point with your tone and facial expressions. Be careful, though; if you stress the same word every time it becomes a pattern, and the viewer will notice.

Let us use the following sentence as an example:

If you like what you see, call us. We want to hear from you.

If you emphasize the word 'you' every time you say it, it will not make sense to the audience. It will simply sound as though you have a strange way of say the word 'you'. If you vary the words and your tone, it will be more convincing. Most importantly, avoid at all costs a monotone delivery with no feeling. It is boring to listen to, and the audience will quickly become aware that you are reading.

If it feels like you are overcooking the emphasis when using an Autocue, it is more than likely that you have got the variety just right.

Speed

Presenters who are new to Autocue often have a tendency to speak too fast, without varying their pace. Another all-too-common problem is the merging of the sentences together, without taking the time to pause in between each one. Audiences need the pause in order to process what has just been said. The trick, as always, is to imagine that you are speaking to one person who really wants to hear what you have to say.

It is likely that there will be an Autocue operator scrolling the script up the screen for you. If this is the case, the operator should follow your pace, whilst trying to keep the line you are reading as close to the 'sweet spot' as possible. This is not always easy and occasionally the operator will need to speed up or slow down the scrolling, in order to keep your eyes as close to the lens as possible. When this happens, try to avoid the temptation to speed up along with the script. If you do

speed up, the operator will speed up too, in an attempt to match your pace, and this may lead to chaos!

A good operator will ensure that the words do not disappear off the top of the screen until you have said them out loud. If necessary, they will stop the scrolling and wait for you. If you are filming at home, or in the office, make sure that the operator is aware that they should be aiming to match your speed as opposed to the other way around. It is incredibly hard to make an Autocue delivery sound natural if you are rushing your words to keep up with an operator who is scrolling too fast.

Setting Up Your Own Teleprompter

If you are working on your own creating vlogs or business presentations, there are alternatives to the full Autocue and operator set-up. Using a laptop computer with the camera lens just above the screen, or a smartphone, you can maintain the appearance that your eyes are on the lens by simply moving as far away from the equipment as possible. When the equipment is a good distance away from the presenter, the camera cannot

Positioning a camera as close to the laptop screen as possible is a simple way to use a teleprompter when self-shooting at home.

see that the eyes are slightly off the lens, and the results can be surprisingly effective.

There is no shortage of teleprompter apps or programmes on the market that can be downloaded. The better-known ones include Prompt Smart Lite (promptsmart.com/products/prompsmart-lite) or Prompt Dog (promptdog.com). Scrolling the text can be achieved with either a hand-held remote or in the form of voice-recognition software teleprompters. The benefit of having your own software is that it enables you to familiarize yourself and practise with the tools at your disposal, which is good preparation for screen tests and auditions.

Teleprompter Fails

Sometimes on live TV there are technical hitches – for example, the Autocue goes blank or stops scrolling, or the wrong text is put up. If any of these events occur, the key piece of advice is, 'Don't panic'. Of course, it is easy to say, but less easy to manage.

If you panic, your audience will lose confidence in you and cracks can slowly start to appear in the relationship you have created.

If a hitch does occur, and the words disappear from view or are incorrect, one of your options is to rely on imparting the information that you do have available. You may have a hard copy of the script to hand that you can refer to. A professional presenter will, of course, have prepared well, and should be able to go off script, explaining the main messages as best they can. If you do have to refer to the hard copy for any specific details, do not try to hide the fact that you are reading, as this would look odd. Instead, make a point of telling the audience what you are doing. Using a phrase such as 'I'm just going to make sure I get these details right' is perfectly acceptable. The viewer will understand why you need to look away and allow for it.

Alternatively, you could play for time while the hitch is being sorted out by taking the opportunity to tell your viewers about the programme's website and content (make sure you are familiar with this in advance), or any upcoming items in the show. Every situation is different and calls for the presenter to be sharp and confident enough to make a good decision. Whatever decision you make, go with it 100 per cent. Showing uncertainty, dithering or doing nothing will almost certainly be the wrong approach.

What you must be careful not to do is ad lib in a personal way. This is most probably not the time to air your own opinions or chat about your plans

Using teleprompter software on a phone can provide excellent results if a good distance between the presenter and phone can be maintained.

for the weekend. Keep it professional and keep it programme-focused.

PROPS

Handling and Displaying

In a TV studio, a prop is anything that is mobile, in shot and not a part of the furniture or wardrobe. It is quite common for presenters to handle props during a programme or piece to camera (PTC), and it is important for them to be aware of how to display the props properly.

Generally, there will be two or more shots of the same prop using different cameras. The first shot will be of the presenter holding the prop and the second will be close up on the prop itself.

When holding a prop for a close-up shot, it is important to hold it as still as possible, as even the tiniest movement will translate to large, unsteady wobbling when seen on the screen. If the scenario allows for it, try resting your hands on a podium or table. This will help steady the shot and prevent any swaying. You might also need to hold the prop in place for longer than seems natural. This is to give the camera operator time to find and focus in on the item and then for the gallery to call the shot. Only then will the audience see it.

Another consideration when presenting props is to be aware of what the camera – and therefore the viewer – can see. If you are describing a prop or showing a picture, it will seem unnatural if you have the item facing away from you. You may, therefore, have to lean forward, look downwards and over the top or try looking around the side. It may feel awkward, but it is important to keep the shot for the audience.

At this point It does not matter if you break eye contact with the audience or that you are peering over the top of the item, attempting to see it, with the top of your head towards the camera. The main aim here is to make sure that the image being broadcast is a beautiful, still shot of the prop.

You might need to point out certain details or features on the prop. When you do this, make any movements deliberate and slow. Quick movements come across as just flashes on the screen when in a close-up shot.

Some studios will have a monitor for the presenter, allowing them to see clearly any items that they are showing to the camera. You might think this would make the process easier. However, you will be required to invert the image in your head – what is on your left will be showing to the audience on the right of the screen and vice versa. The camera does not create a mirror image and this can be very disorienting.

The first shot of a prop will generally be a mid shot, but if there are small details to be shown a close-up will be needed.

The presenter must hold a prop in a very deliberate way when waiting for a close-up shot, keeping it still long enough for the camera and audience to focus and register the details.

Close-up shots can be unforgiving so it is important to ensure nails and skin are well looked after.

Care for Your Hands

Finally, do not forget your hands. They might look clean and well kept when they are just in front of you, with your nails neat and unchewed, but it is a different matter when they are magnified on a 50-inch screen. Every detail will be glaringly obvious, so, if you are going to be handling props a lot of the time, take extra care of your hands and invest in a manicure. They will be as vital to your work as the rest of your physical appearance.

CO-PRESENTING

When presenting with another talent, imagine having a three-way conversation, where two of you (you and the co-presenter) attended an event, but the third person (the viewer) did not. In this scenario you would mainly address the friend who was absent from the event as you were explaining the details, with occasional looks for a reaction or an agreement to the friend who was there. Your job as the presenter is to fill the third person (the viewer) in on the scenario that you and your co-presenter are both aware of. As you do this, you can glance over every so often at your co-presenter, just as you would if the three of you were having a conversation. When it is your co-presenter's turn to talk, look at them and listen to what they are saying. You may occasionally look to the third person (the camera) for a reaction, but the main focus should be on the person who is speaking.

This situation is slightly different when you are co-presenting and you are both using the Autocue. This is because, even when you are not speaking, you will need to keep an eye on the script to ensure you do not miss your part. The Autocue script will display your name, and any other instructions, written in block capitals and possibly underlined. It goes without saying that these words are not to be read out.

THE RUNNING ORDER

The running order is a document that incorporates all the different elements of a show: who is saying what, where they are saying it and how long they

No.	ITEM/NAME	SOURCE	DUR	RX	TX
1	Opening titles	VT-P001	0.30	0.30	
	Intro & link to: Travel Scams	Area A: Presenter-Claire & Paul	0.30	1.00	
2	Sting	VT Prog ident 3	0.05	1.05	
	Travel Scams	VT-Scams 01	3.00	4.05	
	Scam interview	Area B: Presenter- Claire & Paul Guest: Ronny Smith	6.25	10.30	
3	Link to: Winter cooking	Area B: Presenter- Claire & Paul	0.15	10.45	
	Winter cooking	Area C: Presenter- Claire & Paul Chef: Jonny Gibb	4.00	14.45	
4	Link to: Film Review	Area C: Presenter- Claire	0.15	15.00	
	Film Review	VT-Review 01	2.00	17.00	
	Film Review interview	Area B: Presenter- Claire & Paul Guest: Michael Middleton	6.00	23.00	
	Film Review teaser	VT Review 447	0.22	23.22	
5	Link to: DIY	Area B: Presenter- Paul	0.18	23.40	
	DIY Demo	Area D: Presenter- Claire & Paul Guest: Freddy Do	5.30	29.10	
6	Close	Area D: Presenter- Claire & Paul	0.30	29.40	
	Closing Credits	VT-P005	0.20	30.00	

A running order lists every item of a show, ensuring everyone involved knows exactly what is happening and in what order.

will speak for, as well as when titles, stings (short musical clips) and VTs (pre-recorded material) will play. The running order is given to everyone involved in the show. The director and production team will use it as a guide to ensure all news packages, audio and musical interludes, graphics and VTs are entered at the correct time and in the right place. Presenters will very often write extra notes on their running order during rehearsals, as a reminder of important points.

MICROPHONES

You might have heard the phrase, 'The film is only as good as its audio.' The same can be said for all areas of TV and video production. Somewhat surprisingly, viewers are more forgiving of poor visual quality than they are of poor sound quality. However, most presenters tend to overlook the audio and focus on the picture when presenting or self-shooting. The audience will find it hard to pay attention to what is being said if they are distracted by low-quality audio, so it is important to understand the different microphones (or mics) and how to use them correctly.

Lapel Microphones

Most of the time in the studio, presenters will use a lapel microphone, attached by a small clip to a jacket, shirt or blouse lapel. They can also be attached to a dress, a t-shirt or other type of top but this can be tricky, so it is always worth thinking about the mic when choosing what to wear. The small microphone is attached by a wire to a transmitter called a mic pack, or by a larger cable running to the sound system. All these wires and cables should be out of sight, running on the inside of shirts, tops and jackets. The mic pack usually sits on a belt or in an inside jacket pocket. If there is nowhere appropriate for the pack to go, there are special belts available, designed to fit around the torso and underneath low-cut dresses, and other types of clothing.

Never forget that 'you are never alone with a microphone'. Many a public figure, celebrity or

A lapel mic is the standard microphone used for studio work. It is very small and is clipped to a jacket, shirt or blouse, with a wire that connects to a transmitter pack and should be hidden from view.

novice presenter has been caught out making inappropriate remarks while thinking they were off air; in some cases, it has cost them their job and even their career. The lapel mic is so small and discreet, it is easy to forget that it is being worn. Remember also that, unless the mic has been turned off or muted, the crew in the gallery can still hear what is being said by the presenter even after the programme has ended. It is, therefore, a good idea to turn your mic pack off once you leave the set or studio. Never assume that your audio is off just because you are no longer in shot.

Hand-Held Microphones

It is very unlikely that you would ever be required to use a hand-held microphone in a studio. However, you may well be asked to use one when interviewing on location, reporting news from the field or filming at conferences, music or sporting events.

When speaking into a hand-held microphone it is not simply a case of picking up the device and getting on with it. In order to look right, sound clear and seamlessly deliver, you need to be aware of certain aspects and techniques.

DIFFERENT MICROPHONE, DIFFERENT METHOD

All microphones have a 'polar pattern'. This refers to the direction in which the microphone 'picks up'

a sound. There is a huge variety of microphones, but the three main types of polar pattern you are likely to come across in your role as a presenter are the cardioid, omnidirectional and shotgun microphones.

CARDIOID MICROPHONE

Named after its heart-shaped polar pattern, the cardioid microphone is the most popular type for speech as it mainly picks up sound coming directly from the front. It is less sensitive to audio coming into the side of the microphone and has no coverage at the rear. It works best in an environment where there is a lot of noise in front of the speaker, such as a concert or conference hall, as it will pick up less sound from the sides and reject anything from behind. The downside of the cardioid microphone is that it is more susceptible to wind noise and 'plosives' if the microphone is being held to close to the presenter's mouth. This is the tendency of the 'P's or 'B's spoken by the presenter to 'pop', due to the build-up of air pressure behind the lips.

OMNIDIRECTIONAL MICROPHONE

As the name suggests, the omnidirectional microphone picks up sounds from all directions: the

A hand-held microphone is ideal for location interviews, allowing the presenter to record spontaneous comments from members of the public or other guests.

The pick-up area of a cardioid polar pattern microphone is of a good size. It can be angled slightly towards the speaker or held upright and at an equal distance between two speakers.

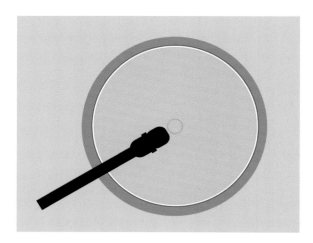

Omnidirectional polar pattern microphones pick up sound from all directions, so can be positioned at an equal distance between multiple sound sources.

front, sides and rear. This means that the speaker does not have to direct their voice into any particular area of the microphone, which is an advantage when interviewing one or more guests. The disadvantages of the omnidirectional microphone are that, as it picks up sounds from all directions, the voices that specifically need to be heard may get lost in amongst the audio coming in from the wider setting.

Shotgun polar pattern microphones are ideal for a noisy environment, as they have a very narrow pick-up range, but they need to be constantly adjusted towards the speaker's mouth.

SHOTGUN MICROPHONE

The shotgun microphone has a long and narrow polar pattern, isolating only the signals coming from the direction in which the microphone is pointed. This means that it is vital for the shotgun mic to be pointing towards the source of the sound being recorded. The disadvantage is that it is easy to forget to move the mic from presenter to speaker when interviewing.

HOLDING THE MICROPHONE

When a microphone is being held by a presenter it is very sensitive to what is known as handling noise. Bumps, scratches, tapping and fingers sliding across the surface of the microphone will all be picked up on the audio. Shotgun mics are particularly susceptible to this and are therefore often used with a shock mount connected to a pistol grip. Whatever mic you are using, however, it is important to hold it correctly.

If you are lucky enough to have a sound engineer working with you on location they may well use a Boom Mic to record audio. This is simply a microphone attached to a long extendable pole called a boom. This allows the sound engineer to stand out of the shot while holding the mic close enough to the presenter to gain a clear sound. Boom Mics are also used by the presenter when an interview is being conducted under social distancing conditions. Moving the mic from the guest

A microphone may be mounted on a pistol grip, to help reduce any handling noise.

to the presenter while using a boom is impractical so the presenter will either wear a separate lapel microphone or they may record the questions separately if it's for a pre-record show. If you do have a sound engineer working with you always follow their direction when it comes to the microphone position, but the general rule is to keep the microphone close and at a consistent distance to the interviewee's mouth. If you are left to your own devices, however, the following points are good general rules

Unless there is a specific reason to the contrary, the microphone should be held in a firm but relaxed way. Holding a microphone too tightly can cause a presenter's hand to shake making the knuckles go white, a clear indicator of stress for anyone watching. The normal holding position for a handheld mic is anywhere around 20–30cm away from your chin and around 20cm out from the centre of your chest. This way, there is no risk of the microphone covering your mouth, which should ensure a good audio pick up.

There are always, of course, exceptions to this rule and when the conditions surrounding you are very noisy you will need to bring the microphone closer to your mouth so that it can capture more of your voice and less of the ambient sound.

If you are using a good quality omnidirectional microphone you might be required to hold it just out of shot. If this is the case, find a mark, it could be a pocket or a button on your shirt, and just hold it still.

If you are interviewing using a Cardioid or shotgun microphone, you will need to make sure it is positioned in front of the person speaking and pointing towards their mouth so that it can pick up the sound. The biggest error a new presenter can make when working with a handheld microphone is forgetting to reposition it back in their direction when talking. This is a sure-fire way of losing half the interview. Other errors include moving the microphone too early or too late resulting in missing dialogue and holding the microphone at different distances between you and the guest, as this can result in vastly different audio levels.

As always, practice is key, so use a hairbrush and get accustomed to the feeling of holding something in your hand when speaking. Also practise moving the mic back and forth as if you are talking to a friend. When this becomes second nature it is one less thing to worry about on the day.

Another thing to be aware of is that guests and members of the public very often attempt to take hold of the mic when the presenter points it in their direction, but never let go of a handheld mic. It is essential that you do not lose control of the mic because without it you will be unable to control the interview, being at the mercy of your guest who may just take the opportunity to put the world to rights. Keep hold of the mic, even if the guest has their hand on it too. It may feel a little awkward, but they'll soon get the message that you're not giving it up.

WINDSHIELDS

Any form of outside broadcast is susceptible to environmental conditions, the worst of which is wind. Unless you are specifically featuring wind in your presentation, perhaps in order to highlight gusts in a major storm, it is not a welcome guest. It is also virtually impossible to remove wind interference in post-production as it cuts straight through the audio. To avoid the sound of wind, it is necessary to add a windshield or wind muff to the microphone.

Dead Cat

When you see a dead cat mic cover, you will immediately understand why it has this name. It is fluffy and furry, and works effectively to block mid-range winds (up to 12mph), whilst enabling the audio to pass through without compromising on the high-frequency response. Sometimes the dead cat is used in combination with a foam microphone to raise the levels of protection.

The dead cat mic cover is a windshield that is commonly used when filming outside.

Foam

The foam cover sits on the end of the microphone and is the windshield of choice for light breezes only. The denser the foam, the more effective it is at lowering wind noise.

Blimp

This hard-core wind muff covers the whole microphone, not just the head. It comprises a hollow cage that sits around the mic, enabling it to absorb the shock and disturbance of strong winds. Older versions were prohibitively heavy and generally required the assistance of a sound engineer, but modern blimps are light in weight and can be comfortably held by the presenter, usually just out of the shot.

The foam windshield is a standard cover for most microphones and is used inside and outside in light breeze conditions only.

The blimp windshield is used outside in windy conditions, often held just out of the shot by the presenter. It can be combined with a dead cat if the wind is particularly strong.

SOUND CHECK

Before getting started, a sound check is essential. When doing the sound check, make sure you speak at the same volume at which you intend to speak when presenting the actual piece. If you are using a hand-held microphone, make sure that the distance at which you hold the device is also consistent. Most camera and audio equipment will have a volume input meter, which displays green, yellow and red lights depending on the strength of the audio signal. Ideally, the loudest part of any recording should just trigger the yellow indicators. If the audio is too loud and the red indicators are displayed, the vocal quality may well be distorted. As a rule of thumb, keeping the audio signal in the top third of the green section will ensure a good audio level without any distortion.

WALKING AND TALKING

Walking and talking is a dynamic way of presenting a piece to camera (PTC). You may be asked to walk and talk if there is something specific to show the audience, such as particular scenery in a travel show or a busy high street. When it comes to walking and talking, there are two standard options:

1. The camera remains stationary and the presenter walks and talks.
2. The camera walks with you.

Camera Stationary

When the camera remains stationary, you will need to work out how long it will take you to get from the starting point of your PTC to the end point. This is done by locating your end point and working backwards. As you walk away from the camera, rehearse the length of time your PTC takes to deliver. When you finish, you have found your starting point. Make sure you finish your PTC at the agreed end point and not long or short of it, as the camera operator may have various camera settings or an end frame for this point.

New presenters have a tendency to stop and start mid-walk rather than simply keeping a smooth consistent pace. If stopping and starting is a necessary part of your PTC and has been rehearsed, this is totally acceptable, but you should not stop out of the blue, without advance notice, otherwise the camera may carry on tracking without you. Also, stopping and starting will make you look hesitant and unsure of what you are doing, which will unnerve the viewer.

Plan in advance how to finish your PTC. Are you going to stop at the point in which you finish talking, or will you stop and continue speaking until the finish of the PTC? Or perhaps you are going to walk off camera. A common transition technique, particularly on programmes with a focus on scenery such as *Countryfile* or on travel shows, is to transition with a 'wipe'. This is where the presenter walks out of view, but the camera shot lingers on a particular sight or scene.

The last point here is to make sure that in the rehearsal you factor into your timing two or three steps before you start your PTC. It is similar to being 'up on 3' (*see* Chapter 3). The viewer should not see the presenter suddenly spring into action from a dead start.

When walking and talking while the camera is stationary, your movement should be rehearsed beforehand. Start and stop points may be marked with a stone or twig.

Walking with a moving camera does not always need a set start or stop point, but you should aim for a consistent pace with no unplanned stops or starts.

Camera Moving

When the camera operator walks with you, you need to be able to keep an eye on the moving lens while walking and delivering your PTC. You also need to keep a measure on your walking speed so that the camera can work with you. This will need to be rehearsed in advance.

Walk with confidence, keep your steps even and concentrate on looking like you are in complete control of both your walk and your words. Make sure you have checked your route prior to your PTC in case of any potholes, large rocks or unwelcome animal deposits. When walking with the camera, it is perfectly acceptable for you to break eye contact with the camera to have a quick glance at where you are going. The audience will understand what you are doing and so will not find it unsettling.

SHOT SIZES

A presenter needs to be aware of a number of different types of shot. In order to adjust your performance accordingly, the general rule is that the closer the shot the less movement you can afford. This is because, if you are on a very close shot, any movement will result in the presenter disappearing off the frame; on the other hand, movement in a

very long shot is barely noticeable. The main shots are the long shot, the mid shot and the close-up.

Long Shot

Often referred to as an establishing shot, the long shot sets up the context or dynamic of the scene or studio. It takes in the presenter at a distance and most of the surroundings.

A long or establishing shot sets the scene and makes the audience aware of who or what the presenter might be looking at, should their eyes not be on the lens.

Mid Shot

In a mid shot, the presenter is generally framed from the waist up, displaying their head, shoulders and also any hand gestures. The reason why this is a popular framing for presenters is because it is a personal shot, close enough to show their facial expressions and authenticity, whilst keeping some of the background in view.

Close-Up

The close-up shot hones in on the presenter's face up close so that the whole background and, therefore, the context of the setting disappear from

A mid shot is the 'go to' size for most PTCs, as it allows the audience to see hand gestures and movement as well as facial expressions.

Close-up shots allow audiences to see into the eyes of a guest and are often used to show emotions or whether an interviewee is being truthful or not.

TOOLS OF THE TRADE AT A GLANCE

- Using an Autocue is more than simple reading. It is about bringing the words to life with variety.
- When using talkback and receiving instructions via an earpiece during a live or as live show, try to develop selective hearing. Practise at home with a mobile phone.
- In multi-camera work, transitions should be smooth and use asides.
- When working to time, finish your script before the end of the allotted time.
- When walking and talking, plot your route before the take and step with confidence.
- Remember, you are never alone with a microphone.

view. The reason for close-up shots is to show emotion – the closer the viewer is, the more micro-facial expressions they can see. Because they are already 'invading the space' of the audience, close-up shots are not commonly used on a presenter. They are more often used on guests, allowing the audience to see every detail of an emotional reaction or genuine thoughts – or maybe even an outright lie.

5
INTERVIEWING

Whoever sets the agenda controls the outcome.

(Noam Chomsky, father of modern linguistics)

During the course of your presenting career, you will almost certainly be expected to conduct an interview. This is an exchange between two people with the goal of communicating a message or imparting information to the audience. The presenter is the interviewer, tasked with the role of asking questions, while the interviewee or guest is the person invited on to the show to answer them.

The word 'interview' may conjure up a memory of attending an assessment meeting for work, university or some other formal situation, but on television or online interviews can be far more than

that. An interview may well be formal if that is the style of the show, but it could just as easily take the form of a friendly chat and include games or quizzes. The important thing to remember is that people are not always watching a show just for information; they are seeking some entertainment too.

Watching a professional television interviewer in action, you could be forgiven for thinking that the art of questioning other people is easy. This is not the case. Preparation is, of course, key, but there are also a number of other techniques that can help to create an impression that it is simple.

Interviews do not have to be formal or serious. They are often fun and informal and can include games, challenges and quizzes.

MANAGING AN INTERVIEW

The Interviewer's Agenda

It is rare to conduct an interview just for the sake of having a two-way chat. Every interview has its own agenda. Your agenda, as the interviewer, is to obtain the information your audience wishes to know about the person you are interviewing. This can be done by way of a 'loose' agenda, aimed at just getting to know the interviewee better, or a 'fixed' agenda, concentrated on grasping a vital fact, overview or insight. Identifying your agenda enables you to structure the interview and prepare the questions accordingly.

For example, if you are interviewing a fashion designer, one potential agenda might be to offer the audience an industry view on the rise of 'size-zero' models. With this is mind, you can prepare your questions so that they cover the practical aspects of zero sizing, the ethical and moral arguments and future outlooks for the industry. Another agenda when your guest is a fashion designer could involve a focus on seasonal trends, as well as what to expect on the catwalks and in the shops. The guest may be the same, but there are potentially two very different interviews available to you and your audience.

Although it is important to have an agenda, it is not necessary to stick rigidly to it. Sometimes, the best interviews are the ones where you follow a line of thought that steers you away from your original destination. Having an agenda, however, gives you a baseline from which to launch your conversation. It also gives you a place to which you can return during the interview, if and when required.

The Guest's Agenda

Of course, it is all very well you as the interviewer having an agenda, but you need to bear in mind that your guest may have their own plans for the interview. They may be an author keen to plug a book or a marathon runner wanting to promote a new exercise regime. Given free rein, an interviewee might attempt to turn the whole slot into either a sales pitch for promoting their product or a soap box on which to air their opinions. While it is reasonable for them to expect a window in which to push their product, and sometimes their product may be the focus of the interview, ultimately your goal must be to stick to your own agenda.

Maintaining Control

If you are to succeed in delivering the interview in an entertaining, informative and/or thought-provoking way, you need to maintain control. This is one of the hardest aspects for a new presenter, especially when there is another agenda at stake.

Guests will often agree to appear on a show because they have their own particular agenda. The presenter needs to be aware of this and be prepared to bring them back on track if they stray too far off piste.

It is not at all uncommon for an interviewee to throw in a curve ball and take the interview off in a completely different direction, simply because it works for them. Often, interviewees are company or PR spokespeople, or celebrities who have had extensive training in 'getting their message across'. They will have a number of tricks up their sleeve to ensure maximum exposure. As the interviewer, your role is to be aware of these techniques, and to step in and take back control. You will need to develop a level of confidence to be able to do this.

One of the most common methods used by highly trained interviewees to avoid difficult questions is known as the 'ABC technique'. This is a three-pronged approach:

- A: Acknowledge the question they have been asked with a, 'Good point, glad you bought that up.'
- B: Bridge the question: 'But before I answer that, I think it's important that we understand this.'
- C: Continue on with their own agenda.

In order to keep control of the interview it helps to have a strategy for bringing the interviewee back in line when they are avoiding questions. This might be by interrupting them with, 'I know where you're going with that, but…', and then adding, 'I'm going to bring you back to the original question.'

A well-trained interviewee might also employ the technique of 'leading'. To do this, they may finish answering one of your questions with a phrase along the lines of, 'But that is not the main point.' By doing this, they are trying to lead you back to their own agenda. They are essentially provoking you into asking them, 'So, what *is* the main point?'

If you want to avoid hearing the main point – which will almost certainly be their agenda – steer clear of taking the bait. You might say, 'I think we've heard the main point. Let's get back to addressing…'.

Remember, often the best questions are the ones that the interviewee does not want to answer, so these are the ones that you should seriously consider pursuing.

Keep it Accessible

Ensure that the words you use in the interview are relatable and accessible to your audience, otherwise you will drive them away. For example, if your interviewee uses an acronym, make sure you clarify what the letters stand for. This shows that you are keeping your audience in mind at all times. If the interviewee has a specialism, the interview might drift into becoming too technical or detailed. If you sense this is happening, pull it back to a more general discussion or, if the points are important, ask the interviewee to give examples or analogies, which offer a broader context.

Nervous Interviewees

Not all interviewees are highly trained media experts. You could just as easily be faced with a nervous person who is not secure in their performance. In these circumstances, you are at risk of having your questions answered with vague and irrelevant statements, a lot of apologies, or not at all. You need to be prepared and ready for any of these instances. If the interviewee is waffling, it is up to you to interrupt and steer them back in the direction in which you want the interview to go. One way of doing this is to say, 'I'm just going to stop you there.'

If they apologize, your job is to put them at ease, and if they dry up and give only one-word or brief answers, you need to be sure that you have prepared enough questions to keep the conversation going so that you can fill the allotted time slot.

PLANNING

The success of an interview rests largely with the planning. If you have planned effectively, all of

The hard work for any presenter happens before setting foot in the studio. The more knowledge and information the presenter has, the greater the chance of guiding the conversation to interesting and entertaining areas.

the hard work will have been completed before you find yourself face to face with your interviewee. The quality of your agenda depends on how much research you have done on the subject matter, or how much creativity you have put into any games or challenge that will be a part of the interview. In this digital age, with seemingly endless sources of information at your fingertips, there is never any excuse not to undertake extensive research.

The more you know about the interviewee and the subject matter, the more confident you will be in keeping control of the interview. Ideally, you will know in advance what message your interviewee will be trying to put across, and you will be able to head them off before they are able to take over the agenda. Also, the more prepared you are, the more daring you will be in terms of pushing the interviewee to answer questions and in maintaining the focus.

The role of the interviewer is to bring the interview to life, giving it energy and purpose. This requires getting the best out of the interviewee; building a rapport, varying the style of questions, having agendas, and providing entertainment, information and, where appropriate, humour.

And all this needs to be achieved while giving the impression that you are simply having a free-flowing two-way chat. Often, the most seemingly spontaneous interview will be the result of the most intensive preparation.

Good planning is the only way for a presenter to create a semblance of calm. It allows you to be ready for all eventualities and means you will have a strategy in place should anything take a turn for the unexpected. Thinking you can just 'wing it', by asking questions off the cuff, is a recipe for disaster. With nothing prepped, the interview will lack structure and direction. You may find yourself on the back foot, helpless in the hands of the interviewee, with no contingency to fall back on when the interview goes off piste.

QUESTIONS

Part of the planning process involves thinking about the type of questions you are going to ask, not only in terms of content but also style. There are a number of ways of asking a question, each of which is likely to generate a different form of answer.

Open-Ended Questions

An open-ended question starts with one of the five Ws: What? Where? Why? When? Who? And the H, How?

When you start a question with one of the five Ws or the H, you are inviting your interviewee to provide you with answers that generally extend to more than a couple of words. Examples might be:

- How do you feel about…?
- What are your thoughts on…?
- Where do you see yourself in…?

Most interviewers favour an open-ended style of questioning because they tend to result in more thoughtful, broad, in-depth and sometimes opinionated answers.

When asking open-ended questions, it is important to avoid making them too open, so that they come across as either vague or too wide-ranging for the time slot provided. Asking questions that are too open is a lazy interview technique and immediately highlights an interviewer's lack of planning, as they are relying on the interviewee to do the thinking. 'Questions' such as 'Tell us something interesting about…?' or 'Is there anything funny that you can share?' are literally asking the guest to be entertaining without any valuable input from the questioner.

Planning your questions in advance will ensure that you can steer the interview in the direction in which you need it to go and will also generate more questions, whilst also providing plenty of scope for the interviewee to express what they want to say.

Closed Questions

If you start your question with a 'Do you know', you can usually expect a single-word answer in reply. An interview based entirely on single-word answers would be little short of disastrous for an interviewer, but such questions do have their place

when gathering facts: 'Do you know how much the government spent on the NHS in the last financial year?'

They can also be valid when a Yes or No answer speaks louder than a multitude of words: 'Is he guilty?' 'Is she alive?'

If you ask too many closed questions, however, the interview will come across as faltering and awkward, without any sense of flow.

Third-Party Questions

Sometimes, you just know that your interviewee knows something really juicy, but you need to dig deep in order to retrieve it. This will require you to ask questions that may be construed as intrusive, personal or contentious. One option is to come straight out with it: 'Why did you lie about the money?' Such a direct approach, however, puts the whole interview at risk of collapsing – the interviewee may even decide to storm off set. If it succeeds, however, and you get a straight answer, you have struck gold. Generally, though, your aim should be not to upset your interviewee.

For a more subtle approach, remove yourself from the direct line of fire by framing the question in such a way that it does not come across as

When preparing questions and agendas, be inventive, and take the conversation to areas where there may be humour, controversy or surprise. Always be on the lookout for an opportunity to entertain the audience.

your opinion: 'There are some people that think you lied about the money. What do you say about that?' It is the same question, but asked in a different way, and is likely to reap better results, as you will not come across as the one making any kind of a judgement. There are other ways to start a question using the third person, for example, 'I read somewhere that…?' or 'There is a rumour that…?'

Hypothetical Questions

Hypothetical questioning can be used to shake things up, by getting the interviewee to look at a situation from a different point of view. This is done by presenting them with a 'what if' style scenario. Hypothetical questions spark the imagination without coming across as threatening, as there is no commitment needed. What they do require is some shape shifting on behalf of the interviewee. If the technique works, it may take the interview off in a different direction, and in doing so reveal another aspect of the interviewee's personality. Examples of hypothetical questions might include, 'If you were in charge, what would you do differently?' or 'If you could go anywhere, where would you go?'

Hypothetical questions can sometimes unnerve the interviewee as they tend to deviate from the main point that they want to put across. As a result, they may respond to your hypothetical question by trying to take control, answering the question in a general way, in order to re-direct the conversation neatly back to their own agenda.

It is also possible to combine a third-person question with a hypothetical one: 'What would you say to someone watching this who thinks…?'

Filler Questions

In planning your interview, make sure you prepare some filler questions. This will give you something to ask when you have just thirty seconds of airtime left and need to fill the last part of the item or show. The questions that work best in this situation are those that are easy and specific, requiring answers of only a few words, and not demanding a deep level of thought or a long explanation. Such questions might include 'Will you come and see us again?', 'Are you looking forward to some time off?', or 'When is the release date again?'

Be prepared to control the interview closely at this point – the guest will have no idea how much time is remaining, as they will not have talkback. They could easily continue talking well after the countdown has ended unless you step in. Be assertive and polite by using a phrase such as, 'I'm going to have to stop you there as we've run out of time.' The guest will understand, as they know there is only a limited amount of time. It is far better to interrupt them than to stay silent and hope that they stop talking in time.

CURIOSITY AND LISTENING

Planning agendas, questions and research is undoubtedly the best way to prepare for an interview. However, a good presenter should also have the ability to be spontaneous, with a sharp mind that is on the look-out for any potential areas of entertainment.

When people are talking face to face, it is natural curiosity that keeps their conversation going. There are no prepared agendas or questions in normal everyday life, so, if something interests us, or does not quite make sense, we simply ask about it. A presenter should do this during an interview too. If you find yourself feeling curious or confused about something the interviewee says, the likelihood is that a good percentage of the audience are too. Pursuing these unplanned points very often leads to some of the most spontaneous, surprising and entertaining interviews, but it all relies on listening. As American entrepreneur and businessman Malcolm Forbes said, 'The art of conversation lies in listening.'

Being able to listen attentively, and understand what is being said, allows a presenter's natural curiosity to develop a spontaneous and engaging interview.

When you are new to interviewing, it is easy to get hung up on the technicalities of the interview – the content, the questions, the timing, maintaining control – to the extent that you forget that what you are essentially doing is having a two-way exchange with someone. That exchange consists of speaking, listening and responding to what is being said. The listening part is as important as the speaking, if not even more important, because it is only by listening that you hear the other person and are able to respond accordingly. This might seem obvious, but it is worth stating. Furthermore, it is essential to be aware that there are two types of listening and that being able to listen correctly in an interview setting takes confidence and practice.

Passive Listening

In passive listening you hear words, but do not necessarily register their meaning. You might find yourself passively listening to the television playing in the background at home, or to two people talking behind you on a bus. If your listening is only passive, it is unlikely that you would be able to recall much of what you heard.

Active Listening

Active listening is vital to the interview process, as it requires you to be fully engaged with the person who is speaking. If you are listening actively, you will be able to pick up on all aspects of what they are saying and respond often to it. You can demonstrate that you are doing this by referring to what you have heard and following it through to a new train of thought. Try saying, 'Can we go back to what you just said about…?' or 'You said you intend to retire early. Can we address what triggered that decision?', for example.

The best interviews happen when the interviewer notes everything that the interviewee says and reacts to it. This shows that they are actively engaged and in effect working on behalf of the audience. A viewer sitting at home is not going to know that the presenter is distracted by all the many daunting aspects of the interview. However, they will notice if the interviewer lets an important point drop or fails to respond to a particular comment.

Maintaining Focus

When the conversation between a presenter and an interviewee feels like a relaxed, two-way chat, they are doing things right. An interviewer who is nervous or poorly prepared is at risk of panicking. Panicking can lead to them not listening and looking down at their notes for the next question while the interviewee is speaking.

Anyone versed in the art of conversation will know how unsettling it is when one party is not looking at the other, and is clearly focused on something else. In the context of an interview, not only is this difficult for the interviewee, but it might also result in the audience becoming detached from the interview, especially if they catch sight of the interviewer's eyes wandering elsewhere.

In order to get the best out of an interviewee, you need to maintain focus and show them that you are actively listening to what they have to say. This requires you to look directly into their eyes when they are speaking and to offer non-verbal responses such as a nod of the head or a smile. Try not to respond verbally all the time. Interviews are usually a multi-camera set-up so, when the guest is speaking, the shot will almost certainly be on them. It can be very distracting if the audience can hear the presenter, who will be off camera, constantly acknowledging their words with 'Right' or 'Okay', or other conversational sounds.

If the interviewee has finished speaking, no further questions come to mind and you have forgotten your next planned question, do not panic. Simply add in a 'filler' – a small phrase that will provide you with a few free seconds – and look down at your notes. Say something along the lines of, 'Something else I wanted to ask you was…' or 'I was looking online earlier and saw that…', then just read out your next question. It is appropriate to look at your notes, as long as it is not when the interviewee is talking, and you should certainly not try to take a peek at them in the hope that no one will see. If you do, you will look as if you are up to something.

VOX POPS

The term 'vox pop' comes from the Latin phrase *Vox Populis*, which literally means 'voice of the people'. The purpose of vox pop interviews is usually not to gather facts but to canvas opinion from members of the general public, and they can be surprisingly entertaining. Unlike the highly polished celeb or politician, with their go-to list of answers and overly protective publicist in tow, the unsuspecting public can be excitingly unpredictable. Where experts give you facts, it is from vox pops that you get opinions and the word on the street.

As always, planning is important. You need to have a firm idea of what it is you hope to achieve from inviting members of the general public to air their views. It might be to bring authenticity to a story, or to obtain a light-hearted view on a subject. Whatever your agenda, it needs to be clear from the outset so that you can ensure it is executed efficiently.

Unlike a studio interview, which is in a relatively controlled environment, vox pops are unpredictable. Anything can and does happen when you involve the public, so, in addition to your basic interviewing techniques, you will need some extra tools in your bag.

Finding an Interviewee

Before you can ask your well-prepared questions and agenda points, you need to find someone who is willing to talk to you. You can pre-arrange the interview by asking someone if they would like to contribute and then start the filming once they have agreed. Alternatively, you can simply approach them with the microphone and ask your first question. Whichever approach you choose, you need to come across as relaxed, likeable and easy to talk to when approaching the public. If you are nervous and stressed, people will sense it in

Vox pops are location interviews with members of the public, often used to garner opinions on current affairs.

a moment and will be scared away. Bear in mind that, unlike media-trained professionals, the general public have had no training and are not accustomed to speaking in front of a camera. Also, they are under no obligation to do so and are free to walk away at any time, should they choose.

If you are approaching a passer-by with a microphone, your first few questions should be easy ones, and should not involve anything personal or controversial. A yes/no question that can be answered with barely a thought can be a good way of hooking in your interviewees.

Once you have got the interview started, you can move on to your agenda and ask for opinions on the issue in question. Continue the interview as you would a two-way conversation and remember to listen to their responses, and engage.

Microphone Technique

When interviewing on location, it is likely that you will be working with a hand-held microphone. Make sure you have a good microphone technique to ensure a professional sound quality. If you are in a quiet setting such as a field or a park, keep the microphone in the middle, equidistant from

yourself and the interviewee. In a very noisy setting, the microphone will have to be turned down, so you will need to hold it closer to the mouth of whoever is speaking. Remember to move it back when it is the turn of the other person to speak.

Camera Awareness

Whenever there is a moving camera in an uncontrolled environment, a presenter needs to be acutely aware of the camera angles. It is very easy to run off in hot pursuit of a vox pop, engage an interviewee and enthusiastically start the interview, all the while forgetting that the camera operator has yet to catch up and can only see the back of your head.

A professional presenter is always aware of what is best for the audience and that includes the optimum shot and camera angle. It might be the case that you have to stand sideways on in order to open up the group to the camera, or gently guide or ask a participant to change position. When using a hand-held microphone, try to hold the mic in the hand that is furthest away from the camera. This will naturally turn your body towards the lens. This is known as 'favouring the camera' and is used in all presenting scenarios, not just vox pops.

When there is a lot of ambient noise, the microphone will need to be held closer to the source of the sound.

If the presenter holds the microphone in their off-camera hand, this can work to bring the body and face around to a favourable position with regard to the camera.

HELEN SHEPPARD: DIRECTOR'S SUMMARY

Anyone can do an interview but what helps to make it worth watching? Whether interviewing in a studio or on location, it is essential that you prepare well, research your material and make sure it is accurate. You are in charge of the interview. Help your guest to feel relaxed and comfortable. Bring your own style to the questions and try not to make them predictable. Listen carefully to what your interviewee is saying and don't spend all the time preparing the next question in your head. A chance comment from the interviewee may lead to something fascinating that you didn't expect.

INTERVIEWING AT A GLANCE

- Know your agenda and maintain control.
- Be overly prepared with extra questions.
- Stay alert and always be aware of what is entertaining for the viewer.
- Remember to talk less and listen more.
- When presenting vox pops, be approachable and be aware of the position of the camera.

6
PIECE TO CAMERA (PTC)

In television and video presenting, a piece to camera, or PTC, is the term used when the presenter speaks directly to the viewer through the lens. It is the most common method for giving information to an audience. Most presenter-led television programmes use a combination of PTCs, interviews and other items to keep the show varied, while documentaries may use numerous PTCs to keep the narrative flowing, intermingled with voiceovers and interviews.

Location PTCs can be used to set the scene and allow the viewer to see that the presenter is right there where the action is. Legendary BBC journalist Kate Adie and her PTCs from the war-torn Middle East were much more effective, for example, than someone performing a voiceover or reporting remotely from the studio.

PTCs may also be used when there are a number of facts and figures to impart, as it is much more interesting for the viewer to have such information delivered by a human being rather than via dry text on a computer screen. In addition, imparting facts and figures lends the presenter an air of authority, giving reassurance to the audience that they can be trusted and relied upon.

SCRIPTS VERSUS AD LIBBING

Writing a script or ad libbing for PTCs is not the same as coming up with words for someone to read in a newspaper or magazine. When we read print, we can take our time to digest the text, go back over it if we feel the need to, and generally give the document our full attention. When we listen, however, research has shown that we engage only around 25 per cent of our brain, leaving 75 per cent thinking about or doing something else. For maximum engagement, therefore, a presenter needs to come up with a script that is punchy and informative, absorbing and entertaining, in order to keep the viewer watching.

There are a number of ways to present a PTC. You can either write a script and memorize it, or read it off a teleprompter, or you can ad lib it. The term 'ad lib' stems from the Latin term *ad libitum* and means 'as you desire'. It is generally used to refer to someone who says whatever comes to mind or speaks off the top of their head. However, this is not what a professional presenter should do when presenting a PTC. When the term ad libbing is used in relation to presenting, it usually means that the presenter is not following a script word for word, but that is not to say that they have not fully prepared for the PTC.

Ad Libbing

For a new presenter, the idea of ad libbing can seem terrifying. You might be afraid of losing your train of thought and panicking, finishing too quickly or saying the wrong thing. However, with the right preparation and structure, it may soon become your method of choice.

One way of approaching the task of ad libbing a PTC is to imagine that you are telling a friend about a holiday. There are a number of specific events

Understanding the key messages of a PTC, and then describing or explaining them in a clear and concise way, is a great alternative to learning scripts.

that took place during the holiday that you wish to recount. Once you have described one of those events, you naturally move on to the next and then the next, and before long you have shared your holiday story.

Relating this analogy to the delivery of a PTC, the events from the holiday example are the key messages. Once the presenter knows and understands what it is they want to say, it is just a matter of remembering in which order to deliver them.

The advantages of ad libbing a PTC are that you can present it conversationally, as if you are simply chatting with a friend. It can also work better when presenting live as it means that you will be open to all of the many eventualities that might unexpectedly occur around you. If you are sticking too tightly to a script, you are less likely to handle the pressure of the unknown. In line with this, it also means that you can alter your PTC to fit in

with any change in direction that might happen spontaneously.

For example, you may be reporting outside the Houses of Parliament and the Prime Minister suddenly walks out. Being able to accommodate this by ad libbing it into your PTC will make for very effective television. On the other hand, if you had been working from a script, you will probably have to ignore the event, as it does not tie in with what you have planned to say.

The downside of ad libbing is that you are at risk of losing your way or becoming woolly. It is very easy to try to over-explain certain points; expert guests, in particular, might go too deep or scientific for the viewer. The rule of thumb is to keep it simple, clear and concise:

The quickest route to the message is usually the best one.

(Brian Naylor)

Scripts

A script written in advance for a PTC allows a presenter to stay true to the information being delivered, as well as keeping to an accurate time frame without missing any important facts and figures.

There are a couple of disadvantages with scripting PTCs, which relate to the way a presenter memorizes and recites the words of a script. When presenting the text, one wrong word can completely throw a presenter, especially if they are new to presenting and prone to nerves. Also, the harder they focus on remembering the words, or on reading them out from a teleprompter, the less expression, sentiment and context they are likely to give to them. This means they are less able to achieve the chattier rhythm that works so well when they are speaking 'free form'. To avoid sounding wooden, anyone wishing to be a professional presenter would be well advised to practise learning and delivering scripted PTCs.

The more you practise something, the easier it becomes and learning scripts is no different.

Learning scripts quickly is a distinct advantage for a professional presenter and time should be spent practising and improving this skill.

Sometimes, due to tight scheduling, you will have very little time to get to grips with a script, so you would be wise to have a method in place for learning lines quickly, prior to taking your place centre stage.

STRUCTURING A PTC

There are hundreds of different ways to structure a PTC. They are used widely across all genres of television and video, for intros, links, content, reports, and much more.

The simplest structure for an intro comprises the following:

1. overview;
2. issue;
3. lead.

An intro based on this structure could be used at the beginning of a report, an interview or a show.

The overview should let the audience know what will be the subject matter of the PTC, or the main points it will cover. It should raise the viewer's curiosity and ideally have some facts or figures, as this will immediately give assurance that you are well informed and credible on the subject you are

---

MEMORIZING SCRIPTS

If you are working with a long script, the key to memorizing it is to break it down into sizeable chunks. Tackle one line at a time and do not move on until you have it securely in your head. The same can be said for memorizing lines: learn one word at a time, then join everything together bit by bit, adding each new element in as you go.

Writing lines down is also a highly effective method for remembering, and studies show that the concentration and focus on the hand movements when writing adds to the process of 'encoding' or learning.

Finally, record yourself saying the script out loud, then listen back whenever you can.

Everybody's mind works in a different way. Some people are more visual, and some are more aligned to audio, so it is worth trying all the methods to find what works best for you. It may well be a combination of all the methods.

presenting. You could begin for example with, 'The UK health supplement market is expected to be worth 15 billion pounds by 2023.'

Moving on to the issue, you need to explain why you are reporting on this event or talking about the situation. What has happened and what are the issues? Maybe there has been a conflict of opinion or a new study has been published? You might continue with, 'But a recent study suggests that taking supplements has no benefit whatsoever to our health.'

The lead is a simple line to take you into the section: 'Joining me now is Joe Bloggs, who conducted the survey, Hello, Joe.'

STRUCTURING A SIMPLE REPORT

News and current affairs reporting are specialist professions and anyone who wants to work in this area will need to obtain qualifications in journalism to ensure they operate within legal and ethical guidelines. Understanding how to put a report together, however, can be helpful in many areas of television and video production as it ensures that the content is delivered in a logical and clear way.

To do this, it is worth sticking to a well-known, tried and tested structure, at least to begin with, while you familiarize yourself with the process. There are four main parts to a simple report:

1. intro;
2. points to cover;
3. conclusion;
4. call to action.

The intro serves the purpose of hooking the viewer in, so you need to kick off with a punchy first couple of sentences. This can be a bold statement, a hard-hitting fact or a thought-provoking question, for example, 'Venice is drowning beneath the weight of mass tourism. Every year, 30 million people visit this ancient city, and the cracks are beginning to show.' In the next sentence, you want to set the scene and clarify the context, perhaps adding a personal comment to connect you with the story:

Using a simple structure to create a PTC is a good way to ensure that no key elements are missed out. As your confidence and ability grow, these structures can become more complex.

I have been coming to Venice since I was a child and it used to be a peaceful, quiet place to rest and reflect. Nowadays, it is more like Disneyland without the rides, the characters or the magic.

The next part of the intro is where you add in the 'for' and 'against' and the reason for this specific PTC:

In this report, I intend to discover whether there is any possibility of saving the city and returning it back to its former glory. Or is it, as the locals believe, destined for permanent ruin?

The final part of the intro is the lead, where you introduce the guest – maybe an expert or someone who is suffering because of the issue – and state what input they can give to the piece:

First port of call is to the Basilica di San Marco to meet with city historian, Francesco DiBilio, who is going to take us on a trip down memory lane as we venture back to Venice in its heyday.

The next part is where you lay out the main points to cover. It is best to do this with some kind of process in mind, so that it is easy for the viewer to take the information on board:

First, I am going to paint you a picture of the Venice of my youth.
Second, we will examine the rise of mass tourism in the city
Finally, we will see what kind of an impact tourism in present-day Venice has on the lives of its residents.

The conclusion is the part of the PTC where you bring all of the facts together and tie them back to the original question:

So, what is to become of Venice? Will the Government's tough new measures have the required effect of saving the city or are we looking at the next Hanging Gardens of Babylon? Is Venice here today but confined to the pages of a history book tomorrow?

The call to action is the best way of signing off, as it in a sense transfers the ball from your court to that of the viewer. Calls to action are where you leave the viewer with food for thought:

Whichever end of the gondola you sit, all of us lovers of Venice have to face up to the fact that this magical city is in dire need of some TLC.

Or you might prefer to encourage the viewer to take action themselves:

If you think you can make a difference, go on to the 'Save Venice' website.

KEEP IT SIMPLE

Remember, if you try to impart too much information, the viewer will become overwhelmed. It is better to say fewer words with stronger impact than an array of empty words that might go in one ear and out the other. The quickest route to the messages is very often the best one.

FILMING A PTC

To make a PTC more interesting and professional, there are a few considerations to bear in mind. (For more on simple filming techniques for self-shooting, *see* Chapter 8.)

Walking and Talking

Some of the best PTCs are produced when you add in different scenes to build the story. You can do this by walking and talking, but you should only walk and talk if there is a reason for doing it – emphasizing the points you are putting across, or backing up your PTC.

Using the example of Venice again, you might start the intro standing still in what appears to be a beautiful empty square, but you could then start walking, to show how crowded the square is just a short distance away. You might move from an ancient landmark to a modern tourist eyesore to illustrate the contrast between the old city and the new. When you walk, keep your eye on the camera so that the audience remains engaged.

Be Bold

People watch television to be entertained, so you need to think about how you can make your PTC interesting and creative. One extreme example is the late presenter Sebastian Horsley, who, in presenting the story of the Roman martyr Saint Sebastian, who met his death bound to a tree and pierced through with arrows, did a PTC semi-clad and similarly tied up. Get right in the middle of the action if you can, as it creates real atmosphere for the viewer.

Take Your Time

Do not rush your PTC. It is a pivotal part of any show – your opportunity as the presenter to connect directly with the viewer and show them that you are as passionate and excited about, and interested in, the topic as they are.

Sequence

Do not expect to present your PTC in the correct sequence, particularly when filming on location. What you say and where you say it is dependent on factors such as positioning of the sun, times of events and the availability of guests. It is not uncommon, for example, for your intro and call for action to be shot in one location, the points that

you are covering to be shot elsewhere, and the conclusion to be filmed in a third location.

Filming on the same subject might take place over a number of days or even weeks. This means that you need to know your script well enough, or have a sufficiently flexible ad lib mental map, to be able to chop and change accordingly. It also requires you to have a good grasp of continuity, otherwise your PTCs are at risk of coming across as stilted and disjointed.

Continuity

Continuity is all about maintaining a seamless flow and the same consistency between shots. It is very important to be aware of continuity because this is not always something that can be fixed in the edit. Continuity affects all aspects of pre-recorded filming. Is the sky in the background the same colour at the start of the PTC as it is at the end? Has the light changed? Is the car that was parked behind you at the start of the PTC still there? As a presenter, you will be expected to remember what you wore when you recorded the previous shot, how you had your hair, with what hand you were holding the prop, the tone of voice you used and your energy levels. Being on top of continuity shows a wider awareness of the whole film-making business, which is all part of being professional, and the shooting crew will be very grateful for it.

Silence is Golden

Never underestimate the power of silence. A born communicator will often feel the need to speak, to fill any gaps, and sometimes to say whatever is on their mind simply as a way of keeping the communication in full flow. Silence, however, is a reflection of strength and control. Someone brave enough to say nothing and wait for the dust to settle gives the impression of being completely in charge, and those who seem to be in charge inspire confidence in others.

Obviously, there are times when silence just does not work. It is not that effective a communication tool for radio presenters, for example. Silence on radio leads to the assumption that there is something wrong with the device that the listener is using, making them twiddle with the knobs or click on the digital buttons. Similarly, it is not effective when working within a tight time frame, with a significant amount of information to impart. Instead, it will put you at risk of running over, before you have had the chance to say what needs to be said. Aside from these two particular situations, though, silence has a way of hooking the audience in a way that often cannot be matched by any amount of word. Silence in a broadcast will unsettle the viewer or listener, and provoke questions: Why are they being silent? Is there some kind of bombshell coming up? How long is this silence going to last?

The more capable you are of adding silence into your presenting, the more confident you will look. Let silence take the place of all the nervier 'um' and 'aah' sentence fillers, which do not instil much confidence in the viewer.

If you are asked a question in an interview situation, do not be afraid of silence as you think of the answer. Better that than rushing in with something spontaneous that you might later regret.

It is easy to feel pressured into filling pauses when being interviewed, especially if a microphone is being pointed at you.

HELEN SHEPPARD: DIRECTOR'S SUMMARY

Ad libbing is a real skill and the more you do it, the better you will get. Generally, no presenter is put in front of a camera without some sort of script. Sometimes the script is very detailed, while at other times it can be simply a series of bullet points. Being able to absorb scripts or information quickly will help you to feel more comfortable and make ad libbing easier. Keep it simple and do not over-complicate, and practise, practise, practise!

PIECE TO CAMERA AT A GLANCE

- A piece to camera, or PTC, involves the presenter speaking directly to the viewer through the camera.
- Scripting makes it easier to stay true to the information you are delivering, and helps you to keep to time.
- On the other hand, scripting can make a presenter sound wooden and rehearsed. Also, they will need to rely on memory if there is no teleprompter.
- One of the benefits of ad libbing is that it can come across as conversational and natural.
- On the other hand, with ad libbing there is a risk of missing the point, putting overly complex information across, going over time.
- When presenting a PTC, keep it simple. Position yourself in a way that tells the story. Be bold.
- Make sure a PTC has something to add and you are not just talking for the sake of it.

7
SHOW FORMATS AND PRODUCTION CREW

The most successful presenters are the ones who are 100 per cent flexible, able to adapt quickly and always prepared for whatever might be thrown their way. Having this flexibility and professionalism towards the job does not go unnoticed, and producers who work on a number of different shows will very often request the same presenter time and time again if they are reliable. So, over the course of your presenting career the chances are you will present on a variety of different show formats.

TV SHOW GENRES

There is wide variety in programming and a presenter needs to adapt their style and technique to suit the show they are working on. For example, it may be entirely appropriate for a performer on a young, lively show hosting a rap battle competition to break some or all of the golden rules that were covered in Chapter 2. The mic technique and movement, in particular, would potentially be very different for this style of show.

Across the range of broadcasting genres there are differing requirements in terms of the techniques and skills needed to present the format. As with many aspects of presenting, there are always exceptions – some people are just lucky – but the majority of successful professional presenters have given themselves the best chance by acquiring all the relevant skills, qualifications and knowledge.

News

The news anchor sitting behind a desk or standing in front of screens in a studio is one of the most common sights on television. If you aspire to be a news presenter, you will need to have more than a passing interest in the news. You should have a passion for current affairs and an in-depth knowledge of world events. Often, news presenters will have started out by doing work experience on a school newspaper or in local radio. Many nowadays will have a degree followed up by a postgraduate qualification in broadcast journalism. The next step involves obtaining experience in the field, as a news journalist, reporter or correspondent. These roles involve extensive travel and the ability to write, present, film and edit video reports,

News presenters are true all-rounders: masters of the teleprompter, talkback and multi-camera studios, as well as interviewing some of the toughest guests imaginable, particularly politicians.

as much of this work is now the responsibility of the presenter. The role of the news anchor is not simply to sit and read the news. Instead, they are often involved in compiling it, so knowing how to write and edit news is essential.

It goes without saying that a newsreader's skill at delivering Autocue scripts, mastered through extensive practice, must be second to none. The world of news moves at a fast pace and demands long hours, flexibility, teamwork and the ability to think quickly on your feet.

Weather

While it is not essential, many weather presenters, particularly those working for the BBC on national news, have had some meteorological training often from the Met Office. On other television channels such as Sky, Channel Four and ITV, weather forecasters tend to come from a journalism background or have worked their way up as presenters in more general fields.

With the BBC broadcasting hundreds of weather forecasts across national, regional and the world service every 24-hour period, working in

this area is a great way of getting your face known. Due to the speed in which the weather changes, most weather forecasts are transmitted live, particularly those that come as part of a wider show such as a segment on breakfast television.

Many television channels receive forecast information and details from professional bodies such as The Met Office or Meteo Group. It is the role of the weather presenter to interpret and expand on those details in order to set the scene for the viewer. Often the weather details are complex, which is where meteorological training helps in being able to decipher the intricate details and relay them into layman's terms. Weather presenters are also required to report in an entertaining and personable style that keeps the attention of the viewer and there is no Autocue as constant reference to the weather map is needed. A strong ability to structure the report using key points and explain the forecast in a clear and concise way is essential. The role of the weather presenter requires precision when it comes to keeping to tight time along with the ability to multitask; talking whilst indicating regions on the green screen weather maps and receiving a continual stream of instructions in their ear via talkback.

Weather presenters spend the majority of their working day analysing data and formulating reports. Actually delivering the weather report at the end of the news is just the tip of the iceberg.

Sports Presenting

Sports presenting is arguably one of the most sought-after careers in broadcasting. Many of the positions are taken up by retired sportspeople: former professional tennis players Sue Barker and Andrew Castle and former footballers Gary Lineker and Jermaine Jenas are just a few of those who are seen regularly on TV. Professional sporting folk have the advantage of having a familiar face, along with practical hands-on expertise and an understanding of all the intricacies of the game that they are presenting.

Many sports presenters start out as journalists, gaining preliminary experience as a sportswriter or reporter. Opportunities in the field range from covering sporting events live – at the top end, that might mean the Olympics, football cup finals, or Wimbledon tennis – to pre- and post-match analysis and sports talk shows. The after-match summary and discussions are an important part of the job and may involve viewers or listeners with many different, or even controversial, opinions. Sports fans tend to be familiar with all the details and complexities of their favourite game. They will be listening very closely to the presenter and commentators, and will not be afraid to express any criticism. It is essential for the aspiring sports broadcaster to devote themselves and their working life to their chosen subject, to gain as much experience as they can, and to make a name for themselves in the industry for their knowledge.

Sports Commentary

Unlike most sports presenting roles on television, sports commentating is mainly audio; the visual will be extensively on the game and the commentator will be seen rarely during this time, if at all. It is a job that requires a unique ability to convey energy, passion, disappointment, surprise and bewilderment using only the spoken word and the tone of your voice. You will also need the ability to watch and concurrently relay what you are seeing to an audience, using entertaining and knowledgeable prose. You are required to paint pictures, describe emotions, know everything inside out about the players, stats and habits, and the history of the sport, as well as reflecting the atmosphere of the

Sports presenters live and breathe their subject. They have a full and thorough understanding of strategy and tactics, players and participants, and all the implications involved in the event of a win, lose or draw.

Sports commentators have a similar understanding and knowledge of sport to their studio-based counterparts, with the added ability to build tension and excitement with their description of the action.

game. A good commentator will always be aware of what is at stake for the teams or players involved and will be able to use that information to build excitement and tension. In sports commentating, there is no taking your eye off the ball – literally. Like a sports presenter, the sports commentator will find their knowledge constantly under scrutiny from the fans.

Shopping TV

Presenters on a TV shopping channel really need to have the gift of the gab as there is rarely a script, with the content mainly being delivered using bullet or key selling points from the product. They also need to be particularly skilled at displaying props while connecting with the audience in a genuine

Shopping TV presenters are the ad libbers extraordinaire of television presenting, with the ability to make everything sound appealing, even if sometimes it is rather unexceptional.

and friendly way. A sales background may well be an advantage, as an understanding of the main techniques of selling is important. A shopping presenter must be seen as trustworthy in the eyes of their audience, so this is one area of presenting where authenticity is essential. Advanced research is also vital so that they can comfortably ad lib to the show's structure without stumbling or losing their way.

It might be that you do not pass the audition for principal shopping presenter, but there may be an opportunity for you to try your hand at being a guest expert. Like the principal presenter, the guest expert needs to make sure that they know the product and can speak about it in a creative, animated way.

Children's Television

There are a number of different genres under the one umbrella of children's TV, so it helps to know what type interests you as a presenter. Are you thinking you would like to present to young children for channels such as CBeebies, or to older kids on CBBC? Are you practical, fun, able to turn your hand to any task and, most importantly, do you love kids? It helps. You need to be able to relate to them and to share their thirst for life, love of adventure and infinite imagination. Being happy to get your hands dirty is a must when working as a younger children's TV presenter, as the role is likely to include some element of making, painting, sticking, and working with both animals and children. If presenting for older children, it helps to have a broad depth of knowledge on subject matter relating to the world of older kids: social media, TV characters, books, music.

One of the greatest taboos when working in children's TV is to speak down to young people, to put on a silly voice or treat them as if they have sub-human intelligence. Children are highly astute and can pick up on when someone is faking it in a matter of seconds. Getting the tone and the pitch right is essential, as is the need to create an immediate connection with your audience so that you build trust. Children generally like to see the presenter as an older friend and not as a teacher or parent.

One traditional route into children's TV is to start out as a studio runner or production office runner at an independent TV company that makes shows of this genre. Many runners go on to become story and programme researchers, coming up with ideas for shows or suggesting possible interviewees or stories to tell. Many of the most successful TV presenters today, including Phillip Schofield, Ant and Dec, Michaela Strachan, all launched their careers in children's television.

Endless energy, genuine enthusiasm and a great imagination make a good presenter for children's TV.

Game Shows

Perhaps you were brought up on Cilla Black's *Blind Date*, or you enjoyed the dramatic ups and downs of the ground-breaking quiz show *Who Wants to be a Millionaire?*, presented by Chris Tarrant. Maybe you were more of a fan of Richard Whiteley on *Countdown*? What you might note each of these presenters had in common was an ability to communicate with the public in an amicable way. They were able to empathize with the contestants' hopes and expectations, and feel for them as they experienced the high and lows of the show, but they combined this with a cheeky, teasing manner. For this reason, many game show presenters have come from a background in stand-up comedy. They have a knack for exciting audiences, engaging them with witty one-liners, whilst keeping the contestants' nerves at bay.

Game show presenters need to be able to explain rules clearly and concisely, but only on a need-to-know basis. There is no point spending five minutes at the beginning of the show explaining every round in detail, as the viewers are likely to lose interest and probably will not remember them anyway. A good game show presenter explains the aim of the game and the main rules at the start of each round, and will recap when appropriate, adding what is at stake at each stage in order to build tension and excitement.

Magazine Shows

A magazine show consists of various short segments of pre-recorded VTs and live studio items based around a variety of current interest topics, such as cooking, health and entertainment news.

Game shows are often presented by comedians or personalities who are already popular from another field. It is very rare for a new presenter to break into the industry via this route.

The presenter will be a true all-rounder. They have to facilitate the introduction and discussion of the various segments, along with news and weather items, and engage in commentary, opinion and conversation with members of the public, experts and other guests. They usually have the ability to find entertainment value in anything from a yogurt taste test to the best high street mortgages.

The magazine show format is largely studio-based and the presenters will be masters of all the tools of the trade. One of the best-known magazine shows is ITV's *This Morning*, currently with presenters Phillip Schofield and Holly Willoughby. The pair share the couch for several hours each week, interviewing guests and introducing different segments such as news and travel at set times in the format. This is a smart-casual form of presenting – it is both business-like and friendly in style. The conversation is relaxed but some of the topics are extremely serious, and may be covered at times in great depth. The presenters tend not to be specialists in any particular field, but are able to turn their hand to a range of subjects.

Factual Entertainment

Factual entertainment shows generally focus on a specific subject and involve a presenter with a specialist knowledge or expertise in that subject. They very often follow the same structure as a magazine show and can be filmed live or as live.

The factual entertainment genre could be further sub-categorized into cookery, documentaries, lifestyle and, some might argue, reality.

Talk Shows

Talk shows are interview-based shows that traditionally have one host, or presenter, and a selection of guests who are invited on to discuss various topics. The host is the face of the show and sets the tone, which depends on the subject matter or theme. This can vary from light entertainment to religious matters or politics.

With an ability to learn quickly and understand the basics about anything and everything, while maintaining enthusiasm and curiosity, the magazine show presenter can always create an interesting and entertaining item.

Factual entertainment presenters have a specialist knowledge of or connection to the subject matter of the programme. Presenting this type of show often requires the ability to learn and deliver scripts quickly.

Presenters working on talk shows need a natural curiosity about people's stories, opinions and circumstances, with the added ability to read a situation and know how far to push a line of questioning.

ONLINE CONTENT

Presenting online video content can be very different from television work as there are few regulations or standards to meet. It is also easy for anyone to upload content with just internet access and a phone and for that reason there is a seemingly endless selection for viewers to choose from. To build a following or fan base online, it is essential for a presenter to allow their personality to shine through. The performance has to be genuine, but the principles remain the same: your presenting style should match the style of the show.

Business

Many online videos will be business-oriented, used for marketing, training or company communication purposes. They can be in the style of a PTC or an interview and very often have on-screen graphics and illustration to help clarify points. The techniques of video presenting very much apply here as there should be nothing distracting the viewer from the key messages of the content.

When presenting on these types of videos, business people are often overly concerned with looking 'professional'. It is important to remember that being personable and approachable, and displaying some warmth, will not diminish your credibility. In fact, it can be used to highlight the most important points or issues. If important points are delivered in a more serious or matter-of-fact way, a certain gravitas will be conferred on them and they will stand out. If the whole video is delivered in a serious or matter-of-fact way, nothing will stand out.

Vlog

A vlog (video log) is sometimes thought of as a video diary and is usually a short video of around five to ten minutes long. Very often it is an account of someone's daily life, travels or challenges, and relies heavily on the presenter's personality to gain a following.

Educational

Covering a vast variety of subjects, these are designed to help educate viewers on a specific topic. The presenter should have a good knowledge and understanding of the subject as well as the ability to explain concepts in a clear and concise way.

Online business videos help companies and entrepreneurs connect quickly and cheaply with their customers and staff. It is essential that the videos offer value, otherwise their effectiveness will quickly diminish.

A vlog is easy to start and is a great way to gain experience in front of the camera, but it takes time and dedication to gain followers and make money.

Educational videos have become very popular as interest in home learning increases. They are very often presented by teachers and lecturers.

How-To Videos

Just as it sounds, a how-to video offers education and advice on how to do something. It is usually presented as a PTC, so strong presenting techniques are a must, along with the ability to explain topics clearly.

Product Reviews, Unboxing and Haul Videos

All of these deal with product reviews and are largely used by consumers considering a purchase. The benefit for the viewer is that they can hear a review of the product while seeing it in action.

How-to videos cover a huge range of topics. They are often shot at home and are presented by someone who has a genuine knowledge of and interest in the subject matter.

Product review, unboxing and haul are all types of videos in which the presenter is reviewing or speaking about products that they have bought or received recently.

Other styles of online video include 'best of' lists, challenges, gaming, movie/book/game reviews, pranks, cooking and self-help, but there is really no limit to the topics that can be covered.

Online videos generally use social media platforms for distribution, but equally they can be uploaded to business, personal or specialist websites. The biggest video hosting platform by far is *YouTube*, which is also the second-largest search engine on the internet after Google. By building a fan base or acquiring and keeping subscribers, presenters can make a living from online videos through sponsorship and advertisements.

FILMING FORMATS

Over the course of your presenting career, the chances are that you will present on a variety of different shows, both in a studio and on location. Each format and place of work demands different techniques and skills.

Studio

One of the benefits of filming in a studio is that there are fewer 'unknowns' to take into consideration. Sound, temperature and lighting can all be controlled, and you are not at the mercy of the ever-changing elements of rain, wind, sunshine, or even hail or snow, or disruptive noises such as an aeroplane passing overhead.

Within the four walls of the studio, a production team has complete control of the environment and can create whatever they require. The space can be large or small, brightly lit or mellow. The team can use green screen or live props, a multitude of stages or just one sofa. The choices and possibilities are endless.

A studio is generally a busy place, with all the many departments and roles working alongside each other: floor managers, camera operators, make-up artists, vision mixers, engineers, lighting director, riggers, and so on. It is a bustling environment, with everyone going about their own business but working as a team to produce the best show.

Running a studio is a very expensive business, especially if there is rent to be paid, so time is limited and every minute has to count. As the presenter, you need to be professional at all times and know exactly what you are doing, so that no time is wasted on excessive retakes. Due to the time and money restrictions, stress levels tend to be higher in a studio, due to the pressure of everyone working against the clock.

Outside Broadcasting

The term 'outside broadcasting', or OB, refers to the remote filming of a live broadcast. It could be at a sports match, outside Number 10 Downing Street or at the scene of a major incident. It may

TV and video studios range from large multi-camera sound stages to a small room with a basic green screen.

well be played numerous times throughout the day on twenty-four-hour news channels, but the fact that you are in the centre of the action, telling the story as it happens, is the main reason for an OB. It is impossible to replicate the atmosphere of a protest march, a rocket launch or the imminent announcement of a royal baby inside a studio, even with green-screen technology.

An 'outside' broadcast is not necessarily recorded out of doors; the term just means that it is away from the studio. It can still be a big operation involving multi-camera set-ups and a mobile gallery located inside a large trailer.

Location

Location filming is used to produce pre-recorded content for broadcast at a later date. This content may be used for documentaries, news stories, special features and VTs.

Presenting on location can be much more intimate than presenting in a big and busy studio, as the team is generally much smaller. Often, there is just the presenter and a camera operator, so it offers a great opportunity to build a rapport and work together as a team. This is your chance to get creative, scouting out the best locations and coming up with ideas for the best shots. When working with a multi-camera set-up, the shots will be mixed together live. On location, however, the camera operator will set up and record one shot, cut it and then set up elsewhere for another. The recorded material will then be edited together at a later date. The benefit of this from the presenting point of view is that you have time in between each shot to familiarize yourself with the upcoming script, to stop off, have a drink, warm your hands. Also, the shots can be much more spontaneous, with new camera positions and locations being found on the hoof as and when new ideas spring to mind.

As you are much more on your own on location, you will not necessarily have a make-up artist or a producer on site, so, apart from having to do your own make-up and costume, you will need to have the means to check your appearance. If you have a mirror with you, you will not have to rely on your camera operator to tell you how you look.

Outside broadcasts (OBs) are live reports from a location where something has happened, or may be about to happen.

Location filming is often scripted and filmed several times before being edited and then used at a later date.

PRODUCTION TEAM

It might appear (in fact, it *should* appear) to the viewer at home that the TV show they are watching is simply the presenter, or presenters, and any guests, chatting in a studio. In reality, however, there is a whole team of individuals who make up the production crew, each playing an invaluable role in bringing the show to life.

Below is an overview of the members of the crew that you will most likely be working alongside when presenting a show. Bear in mind that every production is different and sometimes one person may perform two or three of the roles, especially if the budget is limited. With outside broadcasts, or

if you are vlogging at home, the size of the team will also vary – indeed, there may be no team at all. The following roles are more likely to be the norm when filming inside a larger TV studio.

Director

It is the role of the director to fulfil the vision conceived by the writer and/or producer and bring the show to life. The director works in partnership with the creative team – designers, lighting, sound camera, choreography – but ultimately it is their responsibility to decide on the 'look' of the show. A good director knows in advance exactly what they hope to achieve from the shoot, and how to achieve it. The best directors are excellent communicators with crew, and efficient with what they film whilst at the same time ensuring a natural flow of creativity and entertainment.

When filming in a studio using multiple cameras, the director is based in the gallery working closely with the vision mixers while liaising via talk-back with the technical crew on the studio floor. Whether working with multi cameras in a studio or a single camera on a documentary shoot, their role is to cue all the shots and make the decision in advance, working with camera operators, on how to film the show, what to film and what types of camera position to use.

In a large studio or location there are often far more people working behind the camera than in front of it.

All directors vary in their approach to filming. Some are collaborative, others work alone, some offer feedback, others keep contact to the minimum. Regardless of their style, there is always an expectation that the team will adapt to whatever the director brings to the show.

Sometimes on a live show the role of 'director' as described here is referred to as producer. The aspiring presenter will need to learn to adapt.

Vision Mixer

Working closely with the director, the vision mixer is responsible for deciding which camera feeds, graphics, recorded sequences and replays to transmit during live broadcasts and in what sequence. Located in the gallery in front of a panel or mixing desk made up of multiple screens and buttons, the vison mixer works with the information listed on the running order, and with input from the director, to cut, wipe or mix shots together so that they flow seamlessly for the viewer at home. This is an extremely technical, high-adrenalin job requiring precision, quick timing, the ability to work under intense pressure and a vast knowledge of visual technology.

Sound Engineer

Similar to the vision mixer, the sound mixer works closely with the director and the information listed in the running order to decide which sound to transmit and from what source. Working from a sound mixing desk, they check the quality of input and transmit it either live or recorded by way of mixing, cross-fading or balance.

Production Assistant

The production assistant, or PA, is responsible for keeping running orders and scripts up to date and ensuring that these have all been distributed

A larger multi-camera studio production usually requires a vision mixer, who is responsible for all visual content in a show, ensuring that it is displayed at the correct time.

A sound engineer is responsible for all the audio content that is recorded or broadcast, and very often helps with sorting out the mics for presenters and guests.

to the floor manager, studio floor crew and gallery on time. PAs use a stopwatch to time individual reports and whole programmes and inform the editorial team if there is a chance that a segment is going to overrun or come in under time. They are also responsible for a number of practical duties, such as taking calls and escorting presenters and guests on and off set.

Runner

Where the production assistant is involved with the technicalities of the show, the runner's job is to carry out errands for other members of the crew, such as collecting food and drink, photocopying paperwork and generally being the go-to for any demands or requests that they might have. Starting out as a runner can be a good route of

Working as a runner can be the first step on the career path for anyone wanting to work in television production.

entry into the industry and a great way of getting to know the inner workings of a TV studio. Work experience placements often lead to running jobs. Alternatively, the Production Guild (productionguild.com) is an organization that matches runners with productions.

Editor

The editor is responsible for taking raw footage and transforming it into the polished product that ends up ready for broadcast on the TV screen. Working with the director, the editor mixes live footage with video, music, sound and special effects in order to 'tell the story' that the show intends to present. In news programmes, it is the role of the editor to work with the story producer in writing the text for incoming stories and edit the videos ready for transmission, working with reporters and producers to ensure they have the latest up-to-date footage to air. An editor needs to be a good storyteller, who is able to structure drama, rhythm and tension and set the pace of the show.

Floor Manager

The floor manager ensures that everything that is necessary for the show is in the right place at the right time. This includes having the presenter in the correct location, along with any guests featuring on the show. They will also make sure that all necessary equipment is in working order, that props are where they need to be, and that health and safety regulations are being followed.

Camera Operator

In a large studio, the camera operators tend to film on cameras that are mounted on to pedestals. Prior to shooting, the director will give instructions to the camera operator regarding setting up

Camera operators are responsible for capturing all visual content in a way that is engaging and interesting for the audience. They are highly skilled in the framing, composition and movement of a shot.

the shots and which shots to take. During shooting the camera operators will work off a camera script. On location, if working with a small crew, the camera operator will be much more involved in creatively framing shots and will have more say regarding ways of capturing the action.

In smaller studios there may be just one person looking after the cameras as well as performing all the other studio-floor roles. Sometimes you may even find yourself working in a fully automated studio with no crew at all.

Prompt Operator

The role of the prompt operator is to ensure that the correct scripts are loaded and ready on the teleprompter when needed. They also manage the speed of the text roll, following the presenter if there is any change of pace.

Producer

Unlike many roles in television, which last only as long as the programme is airing, the producer is involved in the project from its inception through to its transmission. They have both a creative and administrative input that includes choosing scripts, raising funds, hiring crew, budgeting, writing, auditioning and hiring talent and creatively guiding the show. They are involved in pre-production, production and post-production, and play a key role in the look, feel and fit of the show.

CASTING

8
CAREER STRATEGY

I've never really viewed myself as particularly talented. Where I excel is ridiculous, sickening work ethic.

(Will Smith)

There are no specific qualifications needed to become a presenter. If you choose to specialize, having an in-depth knowledge of your subject matter is essential, but presenters enter the industry by a variety of routes. Some have a university degree; others do not. Some have behind-the-camera media skills, having had some experience in broadcast journalism, or as a researcher or editor, but others do not. Some have had several years of working in alternative fields; some have not. The industry attracts people from all walks of life. Some have a passion to communicate their ideas and others to entertain, but most will have one thing in common: a determination to succeed.

There are a number of questions you are going to have to ask yourself when pursuing a career as a television or video presenter: what kind of show do I want to present? How do I want to be known? What would be my best 'fit'?

One of the best ways of viewing your career as a presenter is to see it as a journey. Few people, however well-seasoned, embark on a journey without first deciding where to go, how to get there and what they will need for their travels. As a presenter, you need to have a plan of where you want to go, what you are aiming at, and what your target is.

GOAL SETTING

When starting out as a professional presenter it is unlikely that you will fall straight into that full-time dream job. There may well be many years of presenting on anything and everything as you gain experience, build up a list of contacts, and earn some money to pay the bills. If you do not have a plan or a target, this may well be the pattern for your entire career, which is fine, if that suits you. Many performers enjoy the variety of work and challenges this working pattern brings, but you need to be aware that it requires constant networking – being in the right place at the right time, getting noticed by a producer, knowing someone who knows someone, and frequently applying for jobs, not to mention being able to cope with the many auditions and rejections. This constant groundwork becomes your job in between the actual presenting and over time it can be exhausting and frustrating for a performer. Presenters who have a target are far more likely to stay motivated as they head towards their goal.

Identifying your goal can be tricky, but it may help to think about the kind of television or online shows you most enjoy yourself. What are the topics that most interest/excite/entertain you?

Perhaps you love news and see yourself commenting on current affairs. Maybe you are passionate about saving the planet or you really revel in celebrity gossip? Write down all the areas of interest you can think of.

Next, you need to think about your own personality. Are you an open and agreeable person? Are you an extrovert or an introvert? Do you use sarcasm and humour in your exchanges with other people or are you normally serious? Maybe you are genuinely interested in the life stories of others or you like to educate or inform? Analysing your own personality can be difficult – we are all some or all of those things at certain times – but you need to try to identify which traits are more prominent in you. It might be a good idea to ask a friend who you trust for their opinion.

Once you have a list of your interests and your main personality points, cross off any clear mismatches from that list. For example, if you tend to have a sarcastic sense of humour and do not really care about other peoples' lives, starting an 'Agony Aunt' style YouTube channel might be a mistake – unless of course it is an off-the-wall dark comedy.

This exercise should leave you with a list of interests and main personality traits and is a great place to start branding your product: 'presenter you'.

Branding

Branding is a marketing term that can be defined as the way that you portray yourself to the public. It is the image that you put out that you want people to see. Your personal brand and your talent as a presenter are what you are selling.

Ask any successful salesperson what they consider to be the most important part of selling, and they will more than likely tell you that it is to know your product inside out. When you think of 'presenter you' as a product, it will be easier to take an objective look and recognize your key selling points. These are what set you apart from the other performers who are elbowing for a metre-square of space on the world stage.

Once you have identified your key selling points or brand, you can design your marketing around

Your brand is a combination of expertise or skills, your interests or passions, and your personality. Having a unique brand is often a great advantage.

it. If you are just starting out and in need of experience and practice, it might be that having a less precise brand will help you get things going, but you should always have that target in mind. In the end, having a specialism may be the thing that gets you known.

Planning

There are many stories of people being plucked from obscurity and then suddenly finding themselves in the spotlight. Celebrity chef Jamie Oliver was spotted when working as a sous-chef at the River Café in London, which led to him presenting his first TV show, *The Naked Chef.* Historian Lucy Worsley became a TV presenter due to being able to answer an in-depth question about King Alfred. These are examples of a few of the lucky ones, but for the vast majority of presenters the route is less clear-cut. Waiting for opportunities to fall from the sky is like buying a lottery ticket as a way to get a deposit for a house.

Your plan should be a written document that lists everything you hope to achieve, and the steps required to achieve them. This may well change as you go forward and that is fine, but writing down your goals and giving yourself a date to achieve each step helps your mind focus on important points and builds motivation. In fact, studies suggest that people who write down their goals are 42 per cent more likely to achieve them.

Think about and ask yourself the following questions when drawing up your written plan:

1. What is your goal? Be specific and give yourself a time frame.
2. What steps are needed to move towards your goal? Give yourself target dates for each step.
3. What are the different elements needed for your marketing strategy and when will they be achieved?
4. What is your budget?
5. Who are the main contacts in your specific field and how can you get in touch with them?
6. Do you need further training in journalism, editing or presenting? How do you intend to acquire it and by when will you have done it?

Think of your presenting career as a small business. Give yourself goals and set dates by which you want to achieve them.

MARKETING TOOLKIT

Casting directors, producers and agents are approached all the time by presenters looking for work, so you need to be clear about what is going to make you stand out from the crowd. One mistake is sending too much information. No one wants to read through pages of text and they will rarely bother. Think about what a particular producer, director, and so on, needs for the job in question and make it as easy as possible for them to see that you are the person who has it.

The following elements will represent a good start for your marketing toolkit:

- curriculum vitae (CV) or biography;
- showreel;
- publicity pics;
- evidence of your online and social media presence.

Curriculum Vitae (CV)

Chances are, if a TV company puts out an advert requesting presenters for a show, they will be met with an overwhelming number of CVs. To give you an idea of numbers, the BBC receives over 200,000 applications a year for work experience. Clearly, this is a highly competitive industry. The first task of any producer or casting director is going to be getting rid of any CVs that look like they might be too hard to read. This, essentially, applies to any CV with numerous pages designed in a tiny font, with no spacing between the lines, crammed full of dense text.

On their next trawl through, they will be disregarding any generic CVs that have not been tailored to meet the needs of the job, but simply sent on the (very slim) off-chance that no one else will have applied for the same position. It is only on trawl number three that they will look more closely at the content, and move to the top of the pile those who are able to indicate relevant presenting credits and experience.

Your CV should be one page long and include some basic details such as height, hair colour and age range, along with a small head and shoulders picture in the top right-hand corner and a list of any credits. No long descriptions of your responsibilities or achievements are needed; simply list the name of the programme, the production company and the director. You can also add a brief resume of any particular areas of expertise and knowledge, and other talents.

If you are a new presenter with little or no presenting experience, you will be wondering how you can attract the eye of the producer/casting director and convince them that you have the necessary skills to undertake the role. The answer is to write a short biography, or bio. Read through exactly what the job is expecting of the candidate and accurately apply your skills to the requirements. At first glance you might think that you do not have any of the necessary skills, as you have never presented on location or in a studio, for example. However, if you think carefully about the jobs, work experience and training that you have done, you may be able to see how they can be effectively adapted to the role in question.

For example, for a job presenting a travel show the candidate needs to have an enthusiastic personality, a passion for travel, and an ability to ad lib, write material, interview and sell a dream to viewers. You may not have any professional credits presenting travel shows, but perhaps during your gap year you undertook voluntary work teaching drama at a school in Sri Lanka. This ticks the box for 'passion for travel' and for demonstrable signs of a bubbly personality, but you might consider omitting the words 'gap year' and 'voluntary' – you do not need to draw attention to the fact that it was unpaid work.

Next, perhaps you have hosted charity events, been interviewed online, broadcast on hospital radio, written articles for the local rag, worked in telesales or performed at kids' birthday parties. Each of these experiences ticks the box for ability to ad lib, write material, interview and sell a dream, or at least sell double glazing on the phone. Again,

Joseph Bloggs

Height:	6ft
Build:	Slim/Medium
Hair:	Brown
Eyes:	Hazel
Age:	46
Accent:	London/RP
Location:	London
Spotlight No:	12345
Equity:	6789

Television

Vacation to Relocation	**Presenter**	Top Notch Productions
The Cruise Channel	**Presenter**	Cruise Productions
Sky High Travel	**Item Presenter**	3 2 1 Productions
What's Up	**Location Reporter**	Turtle TV

Live

Win your Shopping	**Gameshow Host**	Central Commercial Ltd
The Travel Awards	**Host**	ABBTE
Top Deck Travel	**Guest Presenter**	Worldwide Adventures

Corporate

Safety at Sea	**Presenter**	RYAA
Bennetti Yachts	**Presenter**	Platimun Yachts Ltd
What to Where	**Co-Presenter**	Take Five Films

Online

Where to go?	**Guest Speaker**	Podcast
Gap Year	**Presenter**	YouTube Vlogg

Skills

Editing; Premier Pro, Full driving Licence, DBS check, Competent crew certificate RYA.

Contact

Email: Joebloggs@joebloggs.com   Tel: 0777 123 456   Web: www.joebloggs.com

A performance CV is very different from the sort of CV that might be expected in most other industries. It should be tailored to each job, and a producer or casting director should be able quickly and easily to find any information they need.

there is a way of describing such experiences in a positive light.

Do not discount mentioning any outstanding academic or sporting school or university achievements, as these reflect diligence and ambition, which are both strong selling points. This information is relevant if you have just recently graduated, but is less so if you have been out of education for many years. Examples of continuous learning, such as TV training courses, show that you are consistent and keen to improve in your chosen field of work.

Chances are you will write many CVs and bios over the course of your career, each of them relevant to the presenting job that you are applying for at the time. Although your skills and experience will stay the same, the way you present them will vary according to the requirements of the particular role. Your CV for a corporate presenting job, for example, is not likely to resemble your CV for a presenting job on children's TV.

The CV is a work in progress, to be continually updated, tweaked and altered for every job you apply for, and to be enhanced as and when you acquire another skill or credit.

Remember, presentation is everything, so keep it clean, crisp and easy to read. If you are sending a physical copy through the post, use good-quality 200gsm paper.

Showreels

Your showreel is pivotal to you in your career as a TV presenter. It is your shop window displaying your product and is your chance to get seen, noticed and hopefully called upon, so it has to be your crowning glory. Considering how important the showreel is in potentially launching a career, or at least leading to a ten-minute stint on Fit TV, too many poor-quality examples turn up on the producer/casting director's desk. They are likely to be instantly forgotten.

The purpose of the showreel is to show you in action as a working presenter, conducting interviews, PTCs, and walking and talking, all the while allowing your personality to shine through. Virtually all casting director and producers will want to see your showreel before inviting you to an audition, so it is important to get it right.

So, what should you include? Producers or casting directors will plough through piles of showreels every day when casting and the majority will begin with or include a 'Hello and welcome to the show', or a 'Coming up after the break' or a 'Stay tuned'. If you want to stand out, try to avoid too many such stock phrases and come up with something unique. Make it immediately clear what your brand is. Are you a news presenter, travel presenter or presenter for children's TV? Think about what you have got that sets you apart from any other presenter.

Your showreel does not need to be laid out in chronological order. Nobody is going to mind if you show your most recent work first or last, but you should put your best work first, as the decision whether to continue watching will be made within the first ten seconds. The viewer wants to see *who* you are and *how* you present yourself. Do you come across as natural, professional and confident or are you wild, wacky and unpredictable? Most importantly, are you in possession of the three Ps: Personality, Personality and Personality?

The length of your showreel is important too: two minutes is fine, and three minutes should be the maximum. Think about how to edit it together so that it has maximum impact in the minimal time. You could try arranging your clips so that you start off with a short clip of ten to fifteen seconds, followed by another quick clip, before segueing into a slightly longer clip of twenty seconds or so. What you want is a selection of short, sharp clips showing all different aspects of your talent, so that the producer/casting director gets a real 'feel' for who you are within the first thirty seconds or so of the reel.

Avoid long collages and fancy graphics at the start. These might look pretty, but you are not applying for a job as a graphic artist. You are there to present *you*, so focus on the presenting.

There are a multitude of private companies out there offering to help new presenters compile a showreel, but you need to be careful that your reel is not a carbon copy coming off a production line. A producer will recognize the style and locations of a mass-produced showreel and will instantly know that you have little or no experience, especially if the company producing your reel puts their logo on the titles.

When making your showreel you want at all times to be thinking, 'What is my brand? What do I want to be known for?', and adapting your show-reel to that brand. If you want to be a children's TV presenter, give examples of presenting children's items: telling a story, glueing, drawing, painting, singing a song. For news presenting, direct the showreel towards interviewing, reading the news off a teleprompter, walking and talking and work-ing with green-screen graphics. If your brand is to present for shopping channels, show clips of you talking about products, handling props and engaging with the viewer.

Your photos will give a potential employer their first impression of 'brand you', so you need to ensure that they show some expression and personality. A passport-type shot will not suffice.

Publicity Photos

Ideally, your publicity photos would be taken by a professional. Do not rely on your holiday snaps or best passport photo. Also, when applying for jobs, make sure the picture fits the presenting role in question. Avoid sending your most glamorous half-clad shots when applying for a role in chil-dren's TV, for example. Make sure the photo also fits your brand.

Where publicity shots for acting tend to be black and white head shots, with the actor rarely smiling, presenter photos need to be centred on capturing you looking approachable, engaging and chatty, so you are fully permitted to smile. Also, profes-sionally shot presenter pictures tend to be in col-our, and are not strictly restricted to head shots. Mid- and three-quarter-length photos are often requested too.

GEMMA-LEIGH JAMES, AWARD-WINNING TV AND RADIO PRESENTER

My best advice to give anyone starting out is to get some training, mentoring and a plan of action, then go out and just do it! You'll make some mistakes on the way, but you'll learn from them. Getting yourself involved in your local or community radio and TV stations will help build your experience, confidence and networks. It will prove valuable when you're moving up the career ladder and always re-member the people who have helped you.

Network with supportive, like-minded peo-ple, and move away from those with a big ego, negative mindset or ulterior motives, they will tell you that you can't do it.

Finally, one of the things I've learnt on my journey is that it's not always the best present-er that gets success. It's the one with the most dedication, tenacity and a 'can-do' attitude, so use rejection as a motivator.

Good luck.

SELF-SHOOTING

Being able to self-produce good quality audio and video has never been more important. In early 2020 – in the face of the coronavirus pandemic – usage of the virtual meeting platform Zoom rose in the UK by nearly 2,000 per cent. People who had never expected or wanted to be on-screen communicators found themselves presenting on camera and filming at home with little or no experience and often the results were less than flattering.

YouTubers and vloggers are quite accustomed to self-shooting their content and the chances are that any professional presenter applying for work in recent years will have been asked for a self-tape audition. This is where the performer is required to film the initial audition at home and then upload their video, and submit to the producer, online. The physical screen test process is then reserved for the final few candidates only. Production companies and channels save significantly on the costs of venues, casting director and production crew when running the castings in this way.

Once upon a time, having to self-shoot was quite a laborious task, it required you to hire in a camera for a day or to buy/beg/borrow one, often at great expense. Fortunately, nowadays, new mobile phones have sophisticated 4K or 8K cameras that can produce professional standard quality video, but even High Definition (HD) cameras will do the trick.

Filming on a Phone

If you are using your phone to self-shoot, do not be tempted to film in selfie mode as this setting generally produces a picture of a lower quality. Instead, use the lens that is on the opposite side to the screen. This means that you will not be able to see yourself when filming, so it will be necessary either to record some test shots to ensure the framing is good or use a well-positioned mirror to see the screen. Also, avoid holding the camera in the portrait position, unless you are planning to post on Instagram. Turn it on its side to shoot in the landscape position, which is the normal style

Filming with a modern phone can create professional results with just the basic additions of tripod, microphone and lighting.

for television and film. You also need to keep the camera still to avoid any amateurish wobbling – unless of course that is a style you are going for – so you might want to consider investing in a tripod. These are generally inexpensive and ensure a far more professional finish.

One potential drawback with filming on a phone is the lack of settings that a video camera can provide, which can be used to adjust exposure, zoom, focus and audio levels. This can be resolved with a simple app such as FilMiC Pro, which can be downloaded from the App store.

Audio

It is worth investing in a decent microphone. While many phone cameras are of extremely high quality, the microphones have not yet caught up. A video camera may well have a built-in microphone too, but wherever possible it is better to use an external one. When setting up the external microphone, try to position it as close to the source of sound – the presenter's mouth – as you can without getting it in shot. Ideally, use a mic stand and have the microphone just above the presenter's head.

Using an external microphone can significantly increase the quality of home filming and self-shooting.

Try to avoid rooms where there is an echo. Generally, anywhere that has carpet and soft furnishings, such as beds, sofas or armchairs, is a safe bet for filming. Fabric is a good absorber of sound, which means the microphone will pick up a clean sound signal with little or no ambient noise. If there are too many hard surfaces, such as tiled floors or bare walls, the sound may bounce and this will cause an echo that may be picked up by the mic.

Considering that the sound you create accounts for 50 per cent of the overall quality of a video, you would be wise not to dismiss its importance. No matter how good it looks, if the sound is tinny and echoey, it will come across as cheap and unprofessional.

Rule of Thirds

Composition in photography and filming is commonly governed by the rule of thirds. This means mentally dividing the frame into a grid with two horizontal lines up and two horizontal lines down.

When getting into position your eyes should be two-thirds of the way up the screen and two-thirds of the way to one side. Unless there is a good reason for it, try to avoid positioning yourself right in the middle of the frame as this generally leaves too much empty space around the shot. If you are positioned two-thirds up and just off centre, it is generally a more interesting shot, plus the audience can see a greater proportion of your hand gestures.

If you have your shoulders at a slight angle to the camera, you are less at risk of looking like you are taking a mugshot or adopting a regimental pose. To do this, turn your hips 30 degrees to one side (they will be off camera), but keep your eyes looking into the lens.

Background

The background needs to be darker than the subject, which is you. While it might look attractive sitting with a window behind you, the aperture of

Framing with the presenter's eyes in the centre of the shot reduces the visual communication and leaves a lot of empty space.

Following the rule of thirds allows the audience to see hand movements and leaves a good area for any on-screen titles or images.

the camera will adjust to the light outside, leaving you bathed in shadow. Also, make sure the background behind you is not cluttered as you do not want anything that will detract from you. Make sure you remove any cables, coffee cups or pot plants, keeping your surroundings clean and clear.

A bright source of light in the background can result in the presenter being in shadow. Instead, the light source should be in front of them.

Green Screen

If you want to hide your background completely, you can use a green screen. These are easy to find online and can be made of fabric (make sure it is ironed) or paper (avoid any creases). If you intend to devote many hours to self-shooting, you can paint a wall in special chroma key paint. If you opt to use a green screen, the single most important aspect to be aware of is to ensure that it is evenly lit using soft diffuse lighting. You can check the quality of your lighting using a choice of green screen apps on your smartphone.

When filming, be sure to stand at least one and a half metres in front of your green screen, to prevent casting any shadows, and do not wear anything green.

Lighting

The standard and simplest way to light a presenter uses a method called three-point lighting. The first light is the key light, which is usually the brightest. If you do not have lights that dim, do not worry; they can all be the same intensity. The key light should be placed either to the left or right of the camera and at an angle and distance so as not to cast any obvious shadows on the backdrop. It should be above the height of the subject or presenter – this will seem natural to the viewer, as generally we are used to having objects lit from above due to the sun.

The second light is called the fill light and goes on the opposite side of the camera to the key light. This is generally slightly less intense than the key

A green screen allows you to put in any background you choose but it does require a more advanced understanding of the lighting and editing process.

Three-point lighting is a simple way to light a PTC. Depending on where you are filming, you may have extra light sources from windows, so it is worth experimenting to find the best set-up for each venue.

light. It is usually positioned at the same height as the presenter's face, again ensuring that there are no shadows forming on the background.

Finally, there is the back light, which provides definition and contrast, and separates the subject from the background. It goes behind the presenter either to the left or right and illuminates them from behind. This light is usually set a bit lower than the fill light. It can even be on the ground.

Clothes

When it comes to choosing clothes to wear on camera, there are certain colours and patterns of fabric that work best (*see* Chapter 2). Just to reiterate: plain, pastel colours are a safe bet. Avoid anything with tight patterns, stripes and dots or black and white, which can play havoc with your skin tones.

GETTING WORK

The old saying 'The harder I work the luckier I am' is extremely relevant when it comes to finding work in the performance industry. There are thousands of out-of-work performers who are disillusioned with the television industry, and they will try to tell you that it is a closed shop, with no opportunities. There will be a thousand reasons why they are not successful and the same number of excuses about how it is not their fault. Do not fall into this trap. When you take responsibility for where you are, you empower yourself with the ability to change it.

The best way of obtaining employment as a TV presenter is to work the system methodically, take every opportunity that comes your way, build and maintain working relationships and make networking a part of your everyday life. While it is good to aim high, do not burden yourself with unrealistic expectations. If you have never presented before, you are unlikely to find yourself sitting in Graham Norton's comfy-looking armchair on day one. This can be a very long journey, but it only stops if you step off the path.

Social Media

Never before has a social media presence been more crucial to people starting out in their career in presenting. It is as essential to a specialist seeking to demonstrate their expertise as to someone who is building up a personal brand and looking to get themselves known.

It took a while, but now the TV companies have become savvy to the influence of social media. When hiring new presenters, many casting directors and producers look for someone who has at least 10k subscribers or followers. Producers know that if you are big on social media the show you present for them will have a ready-made audience, as you will bring many of your followers with you.

An online presenter can use social media to create revenue through advertising, sponsorship and affiliate links. Having a specific subject matter is very often the key to successfully monetizing these platforms. Ten thousand viewers interested in and subscribing to a garden-gnome channel provides a great place for a seller of garden gnomes to advertise their product.

Which Platform?

So which platform is best to promote you as a presenter? Twitter, Instagram, LinkedIn, Facebook or YouTube? There is no definitive answer here. In an ideal world you would have thousands of subscribers on all platforms, but, in reality, you will find some platforms work better than others for your brand.

A good place to start is either YouTube or Instagram, but your choice will depend very heavily on your target audience. For example, Instagram has a younger demographic – 70 per cent are under thirty-five – while LinkedIn might be a better platform to use if your focus is more on business. Your other social media platforms can be used as a way of advertising your main platform, by pointing or driving traffic to it. If you already have a large following on a particular social media platform, it makes sense to continue with it, as gaining followers is a full time job in itself.

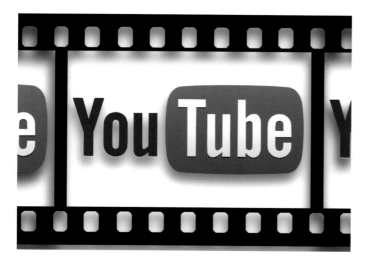

YouTube is easily accessible and a great way to start making content and building a brand.

Setting up Your Social Media

Unsurprisingly, there are countless YouTube videos explaining how to set yourself up correctly on a social media platform, so take the time to watch them through and understand the process.

One key area to consider when setting up your social media is branding. What is it that you want to be known for on your YouTube channel? Is it sports presenting, cooking shows, science documentaries, community TV? Find your niche, build your brand and begin the process of self-shooting relevant footage to populate your channel.

If you want to go down the route of sports presenting, you could take your mobile phone and go to a football stadium. Stand outside the venue and do a two- to three-minute match summary as people are leaving the match. Edit the footage, add an eye-catching title, and a tagline giving your name and the name of the venue. Ideally, go out every week to a new venue and a new match, and repeat. Add in an interview, a piece walking and talking to camera and a live sports commentary, and before long you will have plenty of original content for your channel.

You might want to consider getting your channel an icon, channel banner and thumbnails made up in a way that ties in with your overall branding, so that you start to get recognized. A number of online design companies, including Canva (canva.com) and Picmonkey (picmonkey.com), offer this service.

Create a channel trailer where you, with your well-honed skills as a presenter, welcome viewers and introduce them to who you are and what your channel is all about. Remember, your followers do not invest in the content of your channel; they invest in *you*, the person behind it, so make your personality known.

Directing Traffic

Once you have your social media up and running, looking good and sounding the part, the next step is to direct traffic your way. Around five billion, and counting, YouTube videos are watched each day and so there is no shortage of potential followers.

Titles are pivotal to driving traffic so make sure you write catchy, engaging titles that explain in a couple of words exactly what the viewer is going to get from watching. Some of the most popular titles on YouTube have a 'How To' element or a 'Best of' or a 'Top Ten' and so think of titles you can use that offer instant enticement without the viewer having to think too hard.

Other social media apps such as TikTok or Snapchat allow for short videos only but can still be used to gain followers and advertise your website or other social media pages. Making content that is intriguing, funny or controversial and leaves the viewer wanting more is key to using these platforms effectively. Adding links to your profile and videos that sign posts to your other social media platforms can be tricky to set up as most apps don't like encouraging users to leave their site, so taking some time to watch YouTube videos on the subject is a good idea.

Regular Posts

Consistency is the key, so try to upload videos at least once a week, ideally at the same time of day, so that viewers know when to expect them. Also, let them know when new videos will be coming and then ensure you follow this through. Keep the videos simple, but keep them coming. If you are engaged with feeding your viewers content, they will be engaged with you.

Encourage Interaction

Humans are, by nature, sociable beings, so it is important to bring out the human side of your channel. Try to think of ways to engage your audience, perhaps by asking for comments or suggestions on future topics that they would like to see you cover. All the main social media platforms will display posts more often if they are creating a significant amount of audience interaction.

Encourage viewers to 'Like' your content or 'Comment' on it by adding in social sharing buttons. YouTube rewards interaction by moving your channel up the search engine rankings so, with every video you post, request feedback, likes, dislikes and, best of all, comments. If you can respond to each of your comments, even better. Equally, support other YouTube channels and make connections. If you endorse vlogs, vloggers will endorse you in return. Add in links to the YouTube channels of other companies or individuals. Again, Google rewards outbound links and viewers like being directed to where they want to go.

At the end of your videos, always encourage viewers to subscribe or follow.

Making Contacts

Writing to the relevant people on the off chance that they are looking for a presenter will be a hit-and-miss enterprise, to say the least, but you should not think of it as simply writing to ask for a job. Instead, your long-term goal should be to build relationships and get your name out there. Always be courteous and do not be too pushy. It is a fine balance and sometimes difficult to judge as everyone has a different perception about the right place to draw the line. Remember that, if this is where you are starting to build a reputation, you need to make sure it is a good one.

WHO TO CONTACT?
Based on where you are in your presenting career, start by making a realistic assessment of the kind of shows that you might be in with a chance to present. There are thousands of TV shows available across many channels and broadcasters, including Sky, Virgin and numerous other platforms. Get yourself in front of one of these and spend a morning scrolling through. Locate the type of shows that appear to suit best your level and style of presenting and make a note of them. You might have Sky TV, for example, with 900 channels; browse through them and, if you find a programme you like the look of that fits your brand and/or expertise and has presenters who match your age/gender/style of presentation, take a note of the production company and the name of

the producer in the credits. If it is a live and interactive channel, like some shopping, quiz, psychic or legal channels, it is unlikely to have titles with producers' names. This is easily resolved by carrying out an online search. You can then call the production company and request the name of the recruiting contact, so you know whom to write to.

WHAT TO WRITE
If you start your email or letter with 'Dear Sir/Madam', it is extremely likely to end up being instantly deleted or being thrown in the bin by a PA.

Instead, start your letter with a positive observation about the show you are interested in. Tell the producer or casting director what it is about the show that has attracted your attention and add in some detail that proves not only that you have watched it, but also that you have understood the concept. You might be surprised at the number of people who apply for presenting jobs without ever actually watching the show they are applying for. It is very effective if the compliment you give the production team segues neatly into your own personal introduction. For example, if you are writing to the producer of a cookery show, you might include the something like the following:

> The inventive way that you present the dishes really caught my eye as, having worked as a chef for over 15 years, I place great value on the saying, 'The first bite is with the eye'.

In that one sentence you have done three things: you have highlighted that you have watched the show, you have succeeded in introducing your expertise, and you have dropped in a subtle compliment. From here you could add that you feel your presenting style would fit in nicely with the current line-up of presenters, before elaborating on any unique methods or dishes you may have created. State that you are interested in any opportunities that may arise on the show and would very much appreciate any feedback on the showreel you have attached or enclosed.

This initial communication will almost certainly not land you a job, unless you are very lucky, but it is the first step to building a relationship with the producer. You are now 'on their radar', not as a wannabe writing generic letters with standard words that could apply to any show across the board, but as a professional with a specific interest.

After dealing with a specific show that you feel is a fit for you, identify all the companies producing the type of content that you would like to work on. Your next step is to write to them, targeting your letters so that they are personable and informative. Once these have been sent out, the probability is that nothing will happen. No feedback. Nothing. That is OK. Be prepared for it. It is all part of the process when applying to a production company 'cold'.

Instead of viewing these companies as no-gos and crossing them off your list, write to them again in a couple of months or so with an update:

Since I last contacted you, I have been co-presenting a food and travel show [no need to tell them it was for your own YouTube channel at this point]. I have updated my CV and added the clip to my showreel.

There is a chance that they will think, 'Oh yes, I remember this person.' Once again, it is unlikely anything will happen, but you are putting some seeds in the ground. Keep sending updates to six or seven channels or companies every time you do another presenting job or project and, sooner or later, your commitment and hard work might just pay off.

Of course, 'cold calling' in this way is a difficult route. It is tough to be constantly rejected for your efforts and that is why many people stop persevering. They find it too demoralizing. What you have to remember, however, is that it is not a personal snub. It is just that your brand, your style, or your lack of experience do not fit what the producer or director is looking for at that time. Things do change, though. A new

director or producer may come in and alter the look and feel of the show and, if you continue sending progress reports and keeping the lines of communication open, the fresh eyes may see you as a potential new presenter. The director or producer who has moved on may also remember you and might just consider you for their new project.

The presenters you see on your screen who are 'living the dream' are not there because of luck, but out of perseverance. They have kept their name circulating and, in doing so, have created their luck.

EMAILS OR LETTERS

The way most people today undertake official communication is by way of email. It is quick, efficient and generally elicits a fairly speedy response – unless you are cold calling producers to ask for presenting jobs! The problem with email when sending out showreels, publicity photos and CVs, however, is that they will need to be accessed by way of a link. The time-pressed recipient of the email will be asked to take another step and clink on that link in order to view your work. There are two issues here: first, you are expecting a complete stranger to stop what they are doing and access some files to take a look at someone they know nothing about; and second, and perhaps more importantly, there will be the inevitable concern in their mind that clicking on your link could lead to a computer virus.

Emails are also very quick and easy to delete. If only there was a better way...

If you want to be sure that your letter and marketing toolkit arrive and are seen by someone, jump the queue and send it 'old school': write a letter, print it up, put it in an envelope and handwrite the name and address. It is unusual to receive many handwritten letters in the post these days, so the novelty value of your communication may make the producer or director sufficiently curious to open it.

With your covering letter you should enclose your CV, featuring your brief bio and publicity photo, and a wafer-thin USB stick or other storage device with your showreel on it. The fact that it is a physical object with your name attached instantly places you on their radar.

After your first letter, wait a few months and then write again. You might receive a response after a few attempts, asking you to stop sending the letters. If you do, try to view it positively. At least you have had a response. You could use it as an opportunity to ask what aspect of your presenting was not quite right for their show – you might gain some valuable feedback. They might say that they simply are not recruiting at the moment. If that is the case, you can make a note to write to them again in six months or one year, when their situation may have changed.

The point is to never give up and to use any kind of feedback to learn about yourself and the industry. The more you learn, the more you progress, and the closer this takes you to getting it right the next time.

Standing Out

> Break the rules, not the law, but break the rules.
> *(Arnold Schwarzenegger)*

Sending a hand-addressed letter will separate you from the majority of new presenters, who will have opted to send generic cold-calling emails. But, to make yourself stand out even more, what about enclosing a personalized video instead of a covering letter? You are, after all, applying for a presenting job, so why not let them see what you look like and how you sound? Video processes 60,000 times faster in the brain than text, so it enables you to make an instant impact.

The best way of sending a video is via a video calling card. This is essentially a slim video brochure the size of a mobile phone. When the brochure is opened, the LCD screen inside lights up and starts playing the video.

When recording a video, make sure you refer to the person you are presenting to by name: 'Hi Sue. We haven't met but....' By referring to her by name, you have immediately grabbed her attention. Keep the video to forty seconds maximum, but make sure you provide an overview of who you are and what you do, and, most importantly, pack it full of personality. This is clever. It is a form of thinking out of the box (literally) and it will get you noticed. Sending a video brochure is of course more expensive than simply firing off an email, but they are vastly more effective too. For more details on this method, see the website presenteracademy.com.

If you are the adventurous type, why stop there? With a bit of imagination and creativity there are

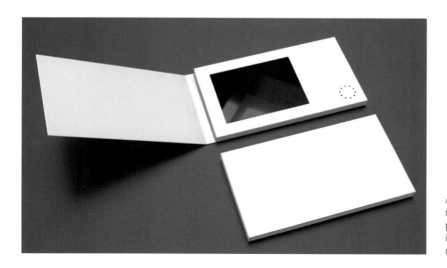

A video brochure, with a recorded message that is specific to each producer and a showreel included, is a great way to stand out and get noticed.

many ways to get 'brand you' noticed. You may have heard of the YouTuber who parked his CV-adorned car outside BBC Radio 1's studio. He had also painted a QR code on the car, which was a link to a video pitching his ideas for a new radio feature; needless to say, he got noticed.

Be creative, use your imagination and break the rules.

Networking

Another way to go above and beyond in order to stand out, and get your name where you want it to be, is to network. Networking is a great way of meeting people, but it does take energy, commitment, and guts – especially if you are the only one in the room who does not already know someone.

Networking events happen all the time up and down the country, so you should not find it difficult to seek out one that suits your needs. Ideally, make sure you are attending a networking event at least twice a month. It is hard at first, but you will soon get into the rhythm and it is all a vital part of a systematic approach to finding work.

Media Networking Events

You can find out about media networking events in your local area on portals such as Eventbrite (Eventbrite.co.uk), or you could target career fairs such as the Eric Festival (meet-eric.co), which offers support and advice for young people looking to break into media jobs, the TV Networking Event organized by BAFTA (bafta.org), the Presenter Network Conference (rmg.co.uk) and the Royal Television Society Midlands Careers Fair (rts.org.uk). All of these are a good launching pad when you are starting out, as they give you an overview of the industry, what is coming up, new trends, companies recruiting, and so on.

Do not just limit yourself to performance-based networking events. TV, radio, film, online production, writing and directing events will also be worthwhile, as they will be full of new and experienced producers and directors. Think about your approach at these events: going up to potential contacts and telling them that you are there solely to land a presenting job can look too needy and will be off-putting for most people. Another option might be to introduce yourself as a YouTuber looking for new ideas or filming tips for your channel. This makes you look like you are self-sufficient and simply interested in the industry and its ways of working.

The most successful method for establishing contacts is not to talk too much about yourself but, instead, to ask a lot of questions. People love talking about themselves. Ask people what they do and why they do it. See what makes other people tick. This sort of insider information is invaluable. You might hear, in the course of asking questions, that someone is prepping a team for a TV pilot. They might mention that they need a presenter, and this will be your cue to drop into the conversation that this is something you do. Give out your card, take their contact details and offer to send your showreel over. Better still, have your showreel on a video calling card and show them immediately. The next day, follow up on your chat with a friendly note and/or a call.

Social Media Networking

By its very nature, social media is a networking tool. Make sure that you have your brand consistent across all of your chosen social media platforms – Instagram, Facebook, YouTube and Twitter – constantly updating your profile and posts and making videos on your areas of expertise.

Much of your networking information can be obtained from Facebook and by joining Facebook networking groups. On Twitter and Instagram, you can follow the producers or directors whom you would like to work with. Comment on their posts, and 'like' their feeds. If you do this in a positive way, with a bit of luck, they might notice you and with just one click they could be directed to your YouTube channel, learning about who you are, watching your videos and seeing your brand.

The more you have your name out in the world, the higher your chance of being seen, noticed and contacted, and, ultimately, of finding work.

Casting Websites and Ads

A great way to start finding presenting work is by way of one of the many casting websites that exist. These websites allow producers to search for talent and for talent to search for jobs.

YOUR PROFILE

Most casting websites allow you to set up a profile page with a picture and a biography of who you are, your brand, experience and credits. When writing your biography remember you are selling your brand and this might mean omitting certain pieces of information. Words such as 'amateur', 'unpaid', 'voluntary', 'school play' and 'work experience' can just highlight a lack of experience. There is nothing wrong with achievements such as these, but when you are up against professionals you want to be in with a chance of matching them. You are making a 'sales pitch', so make sure that you present yourself in the most appealing and professional light.

Bear in mind that casting websites essentially have one role as far as their subscribers are concerned and that is to get aspiring performers to the recruiting contact's door. Once they have got you that far, it is up to you to walk through.

BRANDING

As with all aspects of self-promotion for presenting jobs, when putting your profile up on casting websites you need to think about your brand very carefully and make sure that the image you are portraying is true to who you are. If you are, for example, proposing yourself as a children's presenter, you have to be squeaky clean across all of your social media platforms. If they are interested in hiring you, children's TV producers will always check you out on all the channels, to make sure that you are true to the brand that you are promoting. Pictures of you sunbathing in a skimpy bikini on Instagram or flaunting a full-frontal view of your Calvin Klein underwear on your YouTube channel, or one too many posts of boozy nights out on Facebook, are not going to get you the job. You need to be aware of your public image at all times.

When filling in your profile, be careful not to come across as a Jack or Jill of all trades but master or mistress of none. Too often, people applying for presenting jobs also claim to be a singer, dancer and actor. Singing, dancing and acting are all incredibly valid skills, but if you list them all you are at risk of looking like a chancer – someone casting their net far and wide, just to see what comes back. If the job requests a presenter, be

New performers often feel the need to advertise every skill or talent they have, but they risk being seen as a Jack or Jill of all trades. When applying to a presenting job, focus on the presenting.

just that – a presenter – and give it your all. That way, you become a professional at one trade and you will be known as such.

CASTING SITES FOR ACTORS AND PRESENTERS

The most popular website for presenters starting out and new to the game is StarNow (starnow.co.uk). StarNow is open to anyone interested in a career as 'talent' and also incorporates singers, models, extras and primarily actors. There are no restrictions on joining, so it can be considered a first step for everyone looking to get a foot in the door. StarNow is a useful site for getting experience, stacking up the credits and showreel clips, getting to know people in the industry and building confidence.

Another casting site is Mandy (mandy.com), which posts 6,500 new auditions and production jobs every month. Like StarNow, it has a leaning towards actors, but presenter jobs do come up. Its useful elements include a facility that enables you to see if your application has been viewed by the recruiter.

Both StarNow and Mandy are targeted primarily towards actors and acting jobs, which can work for you if you are a presenter and an actor.

EXPERT COMMENT: RUTH WARRILOW, CASTING MANAGER AT STARNOW

A strong casting profile is important when applying for jobs and auditions via casting websites, to give you the best chance of being called in to the audition room. A casting professional will want to take a quick look at your profile and decide if you might be right for the role. Your main headshot is always what a casting professional will look at first, so ensure this is a professional image, and up to date. There are many times when talent have walked into the casting room and surprised the casting director by not looking anything like their headshot, so be sure to always refresh and update yours when needed. Do not use a selfie, unless this is specifically requested as part of your application, and most definitely no filters!

As well as your main headshot, it is great to have a selection of other headshots and images on your profile that can show a variety of looks. You want to make it as easy as possible for a casting professional to see what you might be able to bring to the table. A showreel is also a really powerful tool to be able to demonstrate your skills and show some contrasting scenes and versatility. You want your content to really engage the watcher, especially a casting professional, and your aim is to capture their attention within the first ten seconds! No montages!

Make sure your credits and experience are kept up to date and laid out clearly, so it is easy to read at a glance. Keep your most recent work at the top with the date, so that casting professionals can see quickly whether you have the experience they require – although experience is not always everything. You can delete old credits that have less relevance as your career builds – there is no need to keep school plays in there after you have been working professionally.

When applying for a job, your application text is also very important. Casting professionals do not want to see a generic message that has been copied and pasted from other jobs you have applied for. Make sure you tailor your message specifically to the job. For example, do you have specific skills that are vital for the role? Are you a particular height that they have requested? Highlight all your matching skills and specifications so it is clear right away why you would be perfect for the role and how you match exactly what they have asked for. This is also a chance to show the casting professional that you have read the entire breakdown before applying.

Castings can have a very fast turnaround, so applying quickly is important. An up-to-date profile will give you a head start, helping the casting professional to rapidly access your look, skills and information, which means they can make an instant decision about whether or not you match the role requirements. Keep everything up to date and as professional as you can, and make sure you meet the brief – applying for absolutely everything, especially roles you are not suited to, can be a waste of time, both for you and for the casting professional. Always check the full breakdown of the role's requirements before applying.

If you are looking for a casting site dedicated only to presenting, however, then Presenter Promotions (presenterpromotions.co.uk) is a good place to obtain your preliminary credits. It covers a full range of presenting jobs, from pub quizzes and seminars to live tours and television work, paid, unpaid, and low paid, but all useful opportunities for obtaining clips and credits.

SPOTLIGHT

Once you have broadcasting experience, credits and an agent, you can progress on to Spotlight, which is the leading industry casting platform. Spotlight requests four professional completed credits in a speaking role in film, television, theatre, voice work, or graduation from a full-time course at an accredited drama school or university. It also requests that you have an agent, who will be the point of contact for casting directors.

ITV AND CHANNEL 4

The Talent Manager (thetalentmanager.com) advertises opportunities and jobs at ITV. Channel 4 are always on the look-out for talent, so do keep an eye on their talent pages (channel4.com/4talent)

OTHER SOURCES

In addition to casting websites, you can also find jobs advertised elsewhere online, on social media sites such as LinkedIn and Facebook, and in print in the *Guardian* jobs section, and *The Stage* and *Broadcast* magazine.

Competitions and Reality TV

Another way of getting some industry experience is to take part in competitions and reality TV. Do not imagine that this is an easy way in, however. Reality TV in particular is fiercely competitive, even to get to the audition stage. Generally, these shows are looking for certain personality types that will cause a sensation or controversy, so think very carefully before going down this route,

as audiences do not hold back when it comes to making their thoughts heard. Some participants have gone on to become well-known presenters on a number of shows, including *X Factor* competitor Rylan, *Great British Bake Off* winner Nadiya Hussain, and *I'd Do Anything* winner Jodie Prenger. They were all 'discovered' on this type of show and now have lucrative presenting careers. Alongside the high-profile competitions, such as *Britain's Got Talent*, *The Apprentice* and *X Factor*, there are also many lesser-known versions. These will not immediately launch you into the public eye but will certainly escalate you into the sights of casting directors.

SAM DARLASTON, KISS FM PRESENTER AND E4 VOICEOVER

I got into presenting when I was at university, as it was a unit of my course. From then I did some work with the university radio station. In 2015 I auditioned for the KISS FM Chosen One competition, but I only entered because my housemates had. In this video, I decided to just be as authentically me as possible and, as a highlight of my time at university was owning a hamster, I decided to do an interview with me and my pet. I somehow managed to beat off thousands in the process and wound up winning the competition beginning my professional presenting journey on KISS Fresh, moving over to KISS FM in 2017 and, alongside KISS, joining Channel 4 in 2020.

Some advice I would always give is, be honest and upfront about who you are, and make sure you treat everybody with kindness. You will see over the years a bubble of people in your industry who started around the same time as you, and, eventually, people only want to work with the kind ones. Also, even though it is easier said than done, try not to worry about mistakes. On my first live KISS show I went to the loo at 4am and took the station off air, and then the next day I played the news bed without turning the mic on for the newsreader, for two and a half minutes live on air. In the end, things like that just become funny stories, and no one ever cares about it as much as you do.

Becoming an Expert

As the popularity of lifestyle TV has grown, so, too, have opportunities for experts to get a slot on a programme in which to talk about their specialist subject. Television producers are always on the look-out for people who 'know their stuff', as they greatly enhance a show, either by adding in contrary lines of thought or by supporting straight-up insights into the topics being discussed.

Becoming a successful guest expert requires more than simply knowing your specialist subject inside out. You need to be able to prove your ability to present it coherently in an entertaining, passionate manner, putting across the facts and figures engagingly. As an expert, you have a responsibility to ensure that the information and advice you give is 100 per cent accurate, as people will listen to you and heed your words as a trusted third party. Being on television gives you gravitas and so it is pivotal that you understand the power of your position and act accordingly.

Research has shown that experts are made, not born. According to the author Malcolm Gladwell, in his bestseller *Outliers*, it takes 10,000 hours of practice in any particular field for someone to become an expert. Clearly, you need to make sure that you pick a topic that you are genuinely interested in if you are just starting out. Whether or not the 10,000 hours theory is entirely accurate, there is some truth in it, as the tried-and-tested method of becoming an expert is dedication to, and active and deliberate practice of, one subject.

Reading a book on a subject you already know about does not turn you into an expert. However, reading the book, writing notes, creatively analysing the information, reading deeper, teaching others on the subject matter in the book, will all put you on a path to becoming an expert.

Our tendency in life is to practise what we already know, but the route to becoming an expert is to become knowledgeable on all aspects of a subject. The more expert you become on your subject, the more you can reach out further,

Having an in-depth knowledge of a subject is a great way to break in to television. If you become the go-to expert on that subject, many different channels and shows will request you when they need professional comment.

As the saying goes, 'If you carry on doing what you've already done you'll get more of what you already have.' Instead, take action, and invest your time and efforts in yourself by trying new things and learning new skills, taking courses, and starting vlogs and YouTube channels.

making deeper connections. Through persistence and stepping out of your comfort zone, you are more likely to find yourself in the right place at the right time, talking to the movers and shakers in your chosen subject and obtaining new insights and opportunities. After a while, your expertise will become your branding, and this is what you can build upon to create a name for yourself.

To get started as an expert, make sure you have a presence online – websites, blogs, podcasts or vlogs that cover your expertise – and keep it fresh and up to date. You need to be located quickly if you want to be considered relevant.

Local radio is a great way of getting your expertise heard. Listen to your local radio station and see what kind of experts they call on and the subject matter they discuss. If you hear a story you have an expert knowledge on, contact the radio station and let them know who you are and what your fresh angle or insight is.

Write a book on your specialist subject. If it is published by a major publishing house, it will be promoted by an in-house publicity and marketing team. If you are with a smaller publisher or self-publishing, send the book out to television producers of relevant lifestyle shows, promote it on your social media platforms and write newspaper and magazine articles in support of it.

Sign up to websites such as Expert Sources (expertsources.co.uk), Past Preservers (pastpreservers.com), or the worldwide Interview Guests Directory (interviewguestsdirectory.com). The BBC Academy are also often on the look-out for experts and have a number of relevant resources on their website (bbc.co.uk/academy/en).

To be a guest expert you need to be flexible. Depending on your speciality, you can sometimes be requested at very short notice, for example, if a news story breaks and your input is required. If you get called up, be available. If you turn them down, for whatever reason, you will rarely get a second chance with the same TV company. The benefits far outweigh any inconvenience – just a couple of minutes on television will get you wide publicity and respect amongst your peers. The go-to guest experts are the ones who television producers know they can rely on to be on time and to do what they are expected to do, and who are easy and flexible to work with.

Work Overseas

If you are a fluent English speaker, ideally but not essentially with an expertise, you need not limit your applications to the four corners of Great Britain. Native English speakers are in high demand worldwide and Great British Presenters (greatbritishpresenters.co.uk) hires candidates for roles across the globe, ranging from TV and commercial presenters to MCs and comperes, and hosts of awards events and other live happenings. For many overseas jobs it might mean moving to the location. As well as being an adventure in itself, this may grant you a great wealth of presenting experience and content for your showreel, as well as indicating flexibility and ability to work with people from all walks of life. You might also become a specialist on the country where you work, again furthering your future career. Native English presenters are popular particularly in Asia and the Middle East.

Work in Production

Traditionally, presenters started out in other parts of the industry and moved to presenting. Working as a runner, researcher, production assistant or floor manager, or being taken on as a graduate trainee on a BBC-style course (bbc.co.uk/careers/trainee-schemes-and-apprenticeships), will provide a vast insight into the whole inner workings of the TV industry. Knowing how it all fits together, in terms of scripts, roles and timings, is a vital component of presenting.

BEING A GUEST EXPERT: ANNABELLE KNIGHT, SEX, RELATIONSHIP, DATING AND BODY LANGUAGE EXPERT

I have worked as a guest expert on lots of different shows over the years, not just on TV but in print and on radio as well. My main piece of advice would be to keep learning. You can never know enough, even if you are an expert. Sign up for courses, go to workshops, and read as much as you can about your specialist subject so that you can be confident you are at the forefront of your specialism.

Having a website or an online presence is also important. Use it as a place to celebrate your love and passion for what you do. It can be used as a sort of online CV, a showreel, and a place to contact you all in one. Just make sure you keep it up to date and relevant. You don't want to miss out on an opportunity just because you let your website slip.

Having an agent will help you dramatically, but never underestimate just how much your own hard work and perseverance can pay off. Never be too shy to put yourself out there. You may not be right for that person right now, but that does not mean you won't be in the future. Getting yourself on people's radars is never a bad thing, and neither is keeping in touch every few months or so.

I do a lot of work for free. Sometimes I'll be asked for expert comment for a magazine or paper and there won't be a fee. This is common and I always weigh up whether it is worth it by thinking in terms of longevity. Okay, so you might not be banking a fee right now, but you never know what the person asking for your comment will go on to do. I keep to the motto, always happy to help…if I can.

Often, TV producers will call you in at the last minute, or radio shows will need you to speak on your subject right there and then. The better able you are to say yes to these opportunities as and when they arise, the better your relationship with those producers will be, and the more they will think of you in the future.

Many people start in production on a work experience placement or internship. These positions are either unpaid or offer very low remuneration, but they still have many more applicants than places. It is a less popular route to presenting now, as there are thousands of people who genuinely want to work – and stay working – in TV production. Someone who takes one of those places, with an ulterior motive getting into presenting, is depriving another person of an opportunity.

Work in Broadcast Journalism

Starting out in print or radio journalism is another way of carving out a route into the television industry. The major employers of broadcast journalists are the BBC, Channel 4, ITN, Sky News and other digital companies, along with newspapers, who employ broadcast journalists for their online digital content, and independent production companies, who source news for broadcasting stations. It is not essential to have a degree in order to become a broadcast journalist, but having some training in journalism is important. The NCTJ (nctj.com) offers a range of training options.

The BBC's training schemes remain the most sought-after routes into broadcast journalism, and the competition is fierce. The majority of people applying to the BBC are graduates, many of whom have studied a year-long postgraduate degree in broadcast journalism. That said, the BBC is a key employer of broadcast journalists, with several thousand roles, so it is worth staying tuned to the BBC careers website (bbc.co.uk/careers). Another option is to undertake a fast-track training course that runs up to twenty weeks and is approved by the Broadcast Journalist Training Council (bjtc. org.uk). The role of the broadcast journalist is to source and research new stories, write bulletins and news scripts, and broadcast the news in an engaging way.

Using an Agent

One of the most common questions that new television presenters ask is whether they should have an agent. The answer to this is generally yes, but do not rush into it. To begin with, it is highly unlikely an agent will want to take you on if you do not have any experience in front of the camera. Agents

Journalism is not for the faint-hearted. You will need to have a good understanding of media law, ethics and regulations, and still be able to make engaging, hard-hitting and sometimes controversial reports.

spend many years building relationships with casting directors and producers and their reputation relies on providing quality, considered suggestions for the available roles. It is unlikely then that they would submit someone for a presenting role who they have not seen work, on the off chance that they might be good in front of the camera.

The time to get an agent is when you have had a few jobs, or when you are so busy working as a presenter that you have no time for all the necessary administration. An agent will manage your bookings for you and at the same time put your name forward for bigger and better presenting roles, and work on getting your name out into the stratosphere.

Agents come in all shapes and sizes, from large companies who represent many clients to smaller niche-style agents, with just a few choice clients on their books. Some specialize in specific areas, while others work across the board.

The benefit of having an agent is that they know people who know people and can recommend you for jobs that are not posted or advertised. They are often the first port of call for casting directors and they know all of the ins and outs of the industry. They are also very good at negotiating the correct

rates and terms for their talent. Performers often find it difficult to know what to say when they are asked for their daily rate – they do not want to price themselves out of the market, but neither do they want to under-sell themselves. A good agent, however, eats rate negotiations for breakfast!

The best way of finding the right agent for you is by finding out who represents the presenters who are working on the shows that you would like to work on. It is a good bet that the agent will know all the right contacts working within the show you are interested in.

When meeting an agent for the first time, be enthusiastic, show your level of commitment and, most importantly, make it clear that you have a road map for where you are and where you want to be. Agents want clients who have a clear vision of their own career path, who know themselves and where they fit with their branding, and who are hard grafters, prepared to put the work in.

An agent will charge a commission on the payment you receive from a presenting contract. The rates are generally between 15 and 20 per cent of your fees, but commercials can be higher. Some agencies will charge a joining fee as well as taking a commission, but these companies generally

EXPERT COMMENT: KAREN WITCHALLS-PLUNKETT, AGENT AND FOUNDER OF PMP AGENCY

What does an agent look for from a presenter? A showreel or links to clips. The first thing I want to see is how you are on camera. Then a good photo that represents your current look and a bio that gives details about you, your skills and any experience you have had, whether it be professional or not. Also, send any links to your social media platforms. These days, casting directors and producers may ask for these when an agent puts their client forward for a job if they are not already on their client web page.

The ideal length for a showreel is two minutes. It needs to grab the attention in the first few seconds, and you need to be yourself, not a character or presenter like anyone else you have seen on TV. If you do not have a showreel it is worth sending clips or a link to footage on your YouTube, your website or any of the other social media channels you use. Do not send links that are out of date. Footage needs to be current and show your talent, expertise/skills and/or passion.

You can email all your details – or why not try using the post! It may seem old-fashioned, but as we do not generally receive many letters these days it is potentially more likely to be opened and responded to! Always follow up with a call, to make sure your details have arrived. If you do not receive an answer after the first time of trying, do not give up. Half the job of trying to get an agent can be about timing and determination.

have hundreds if not thousands of people on their books, as they predominantly focus on background or extra work.

A good agent will take on only as many presenters as their team can effectively manage.

One great resource for finding an agent as well as other industry specialists is Spotlight Contacts (spotlight.com/contacts), which refers to itself as the industry 'address book'. It lists agents and sometimes the genre of industry that they represent.

Auditions

The advice for aspiring new presenters tends to be that they ought to attend as many auditions as they can. The thinking is that every audition, whether you sink or swim, is a useful experience. However, you should really only start spending the time, money and effort needed to secure auditions when you are at least competent with the tools of the trade: where to put your hands, how to stand, how to use Autocue and an earpiece. If you are not well prepared, there is a high probability that you will mess up and not get the job. This will inevitably knock your confidence, especially if it happens repeatedly, and there is only so much rejection a person can take. Take the time therefore, in metaphorical terms, to learn to fly the plane before attempting to take off. Once the tools and techniques of presenting have become familiar to you, that is the time to start attending every audition you can – big and small, paid and unpaid – and, in turn, the time when you are more likely to secure a job.

The purpose of the audition is to give the producer and/or casting director the chance to get to know you. They want to know who you are, how you come across to other people, whether or not you can think on your feet, stay calm under pressure and engage an audience. They want to gauge your levels of energy, passion and enthusiasm and, most of all, see your personality.

The key to a successful audition is to be prepared. This might sound obvious, but all too often you hear people bemoaning the fact that they were asked out of the blue to give a two-minute speech on a certain topic, or that they felt totally 'wrong' for the part. That is because they have not done their research and discovered what is expected of them. You will receive a brief beforehand from your agent or from the production company, so make sure you understand it fully. If there are items to prepare or lines to learn, make sure you are on top of it. Do your homework and find out everything there is to know about the show that you are auditioning for. If it is a new show, familiarize yourself with other projects that the producer has worked on, to get a sense of what kind of shows they like

Careers are made or broken in auditions, so prepare well and practise. Even the most experienced presenter can feel the pressure at a screen test.

to produce. If the chance arises, remember to tell the producer that you enjoyed a particular aspect of one of their shows. It might sound ingratiatingly over the top, but you will get brownie points for having taken the time to research their portfolio.

It may seem obvious but, if you are auditioning to present a motoring programme, you need to read up about cars, racetracks, cylinders and horsepower, and get to grips with the mood of the show. Who is it aimed at? What is the tone? How do the presenters dress and how do they address one another? Watch the show if you can and get to know it intimately.

Do not be put off by the other people auditioning with you. They might appear more confident than you, but an over-confident air is often a mask for shyness. Do not allow other people to wind you up. Keep your mind on your own relaxation and focus. Whatever the mood and the setting, be 100 per cent professional. It is not unknown for a producer to sit incognito in a waiting room with a group of presenters, just to get a real feel of the people auditioning.

When you walk into your audition, shake hands firmly and look the producer and/or casting director in the eye. This will show strength, determination and confidence and set your audition off to a good start.

Be fully prepared for whatever might come your way. Producers and directors want to know how you cope under pressure, so they may call a fault on Autocue, ask you to talk about something unexpected for a minute or two, or maybe prompt you to tell them a joke. Be ready for anything.

CAREER STRATEGY AT A GLANCE

- Ensure you understand your branding and use it consistently on social media.
- Build up online content of your work on social media.
- Be systematic with your job search and make a plan.
- Find a name and avoid using 'Dear Sir/Madam' in all correspondence.
- Put time aside every couple of weeks to network.
- Join a casting website.
- Up your chances of success by specializing or becoming an expert.
- Consider working overseas.
- Prepare, prepare, prepare.

GLOSSARY AND JARGON

Action: A verbal instruction used as the talent's cue to start, more widely used in acting but also common when filming pre-recorded PTCs.

Ad libbing: Presenting without the aid of a script or scripted words.

Agency: A company that provides general performers to the film and television industry. Very often they will specialize in supporting background artists.

Agent: A person or a company that actively seeks paid working contracts for individual presenters, actors or performers.

Anchor: Studio-based presenter often delivering news and current affairs.

As live: Describes a programme or segment that is filmed as a live broadcast but will be transmitted at a later date.

Autocue: The trade name of one of the first teleprompters widely available to the television industry.

Back-announcement: When an item is referred to or described after it has been played. Often used on radio to back-announce a song.

Blocking: Any specific planned movements that talent, guests, cameras or larger props have to do on set or location during filming.

Boom: Hand-held telescopic pole with a microphone attached, held at the required distance by a member of the crew, who is out of shot and able to follow any movement by the talent.

Breaking news: Newsworthy events and situations that have recently occurred, details of which are arriving to the studio during the broadcast.

Brief: A document that describes what is required or can be expected from a show, talent, celebrity or guest appearance. There are a variety of types, for example, for talent at an audition or casting; for a celebrity or guest appearance on a show; from a client to a production company regarding a filming project; or for an idea for a show or programme.

Bulletin: A short news broadcast.

Buy-out: Also known as a buy-out of rights, when a performer is paid a lump sum instead of repeat fees.

Call sheet: A document given to the cast and crew before the start of a filming day. It includes a schedule, timings and contact details of everyone involved in the day's filming.

Call time: The time when a member of the cast or crew needs to arrive on site.

Cam: Another term for a camera.

Cans: Another term for headphones.

Casting director: A person responsible for choosing and recruiting talent for a particular show.

Chroma key: A process used to superimpose a background into a shot during the editing process.

Clapperboard: Also known as the slate. Used to mark each take by number and scene. Also allows the editor to synchronize sound and vision if they have been recorded separately.

Clear: A verbal instruction often used in a live studio environment to indicate that the audio is no longer being broadcast.

Confirmed booking: An agreement that a performer will work on a particular production.

Continuity: The process of ensuring all details on set and all performances are consistent if more than one pre-recorded shot is being used.

Correspondent: A journalist or presenter who reports on stories from outside the studio or newsroom.

Cross-fading: A technique whereby an outgoing track or clip is fading out while the incoming track is fading in.

Cue: A verbal or visual signal for the talent to start.

Cue light: A light that indicates recording or broadcast is in process, often used in a multi-camera setting to identify the active camera.

Cut: A verbal instruction from a director or producer to stop filming.

Cutaway: A shot or clip that captures a reaction or details that are not the main focus point or action. Sometimes referred to as a B-roll.

Dead air: A term used in radio or podcasting when silence is being broadcast.

Demo reel: Also known as a showreel, a short video containing examples of a talent's work, to be provided to potential employers.

Dirty shot: A shot where part of another person, usually the back of one shoulder and the head, can be seen in frame with the main presenter. In TV presenting, it is usually used during an interview.

Down the line: Describes an interview where the participants are in different locations. Often, the guest is being seen and heard via a live video feed into the main studio.

Dry run: A rehearsal that is not recorded or broadcast.

Edit: A particular version of a film or video after it has been worked on and refined. Different edits may be used for different platforms, for example broadcast TV, Facebook, YouTube, Instagram, and so on.

Editing: The process of piecing together all the raw footage, audio, VTs, titles and anything else that is to be in the final programme or video.

Equity: Union in the UK that represents artists.

Eye line: The direction in which someone is looking.

Feature: A non-breaking story or an item on people, trends, issues or a particular subject.

Feedback: An ear-piercing, high-pitched whistle caused by a microphone picking up its own signal from a loudspeaker or headphone. This creates a continuous, amplified audio loop.

Final checks: A verbal call from the director or producer, indicating that filming is ready to start and any last-minute checks should be made, particularly to hair, make-up and wardrobe.

Floor manager: The person who is responsible for ensuring everything in the studio area goes to plan.

From the top: A term used to indicate the filming will start again from the very beginning.

Gaffer: The person in charge of lighting, also known as chief lighting technician.

Gaffer tape: A strong, wide adhesive tape used for everything and anything on set.

Gallery: Also known as the production control room. The place where producers and directors control all elements of a live or as-live show and create the final output.

Green room: An area where anyone appearing in a programme waits before being called to the set. Despite its name, the walls may be any colour!

Green screen: A green fabric screen or painted background that is used in the chromo key process. A blue screen can also be used.

Guest: Anyone who will be appearing on a show, apart from the presenter. Often used to refer to interviewees who are not necessarily well known. A more famous interviewee will be referred to as a celebrity guest.

Haul: Term used for a YouTube video showing various items a YouTuber has just bought.

HDTV (High Definition Television): Broadcast that uses a line standard of 720p or greater.

Headshot: Publicity photographs of talent used in the casting process.

Hook: A short description of an item or show, used to entice people to watch.

Ident: A short video or audio sequence that identifies a show.

Insert: A close-up shot of an item, for example a product.

Jingle: A short song or tune with vocals used on a programme to identify the show or presenter, or used for advertising.

Link: Piece to camera between two items or features.

Live stream: An online video filmed and uploaded as it happens in real time.

Location: A site or venue away from the main studio used for filming.

Lower third: A small graphic or logo used to display titles and text in the lower third of the screen. Upper thirds are occasionally used too.

Magazine show: A TV or radio programme made up of various reports, stories or items.

Mic: Another term for microphone.

Mixer desk: Technical equipment used to combine various live and pre-recorded video and audio clips together.

Multi-camera: Also called multiple-camera set-up or simply multi-cam. A way of filming a scene using a combination of shots from several cameras.

Noddy: Cutaway of a presenter or listener reacting to what is being said.

OB: Outside broadcast.

OFCOM: Office of Communications. The regulator of broadcasting and communications in the UK.

OOV (out of vision) video: Describes a shot when a presenter is talking, but cannot be seen on the screen. The visual will be images or video relevant to what is being said.

Pan: A camera movement or turn, which can be horizontal or vertical.

Pencil/pencilled in: Before a job is confirmed, a talent may get a pencil or be pencilled in. This means that they have been shortlisted.

Pick-ups: Small or short pieces of footage that are usually filmed after the main shot has been done. They might be quick shots to fill in details, close-ups of props or cutaway shots.

Pilot: A one-off episode of a proposed series to test the reaction of the audience and to gauge the viability of the series.

PM (production manager): The person who controls the production budgets, funding, staffing and health and safety. The PM needs to have an understanding of both the creative and technical aspects of production.

Popping: Distorted audio caused by a mic being too close to a presenter's mouth.

POV (point of view): Shot where the camera takes the viewpoint of the presenter.

Pre-record: Footage or audio that is recorded and edited in advance before broadcast.

Producer: The person who coordinates, supervises and controls major aspects of a television or video project.

Prospects: A list of possible stories to include in a news programme.

PTC (piece to camera): Any shot where the presenter speaks directly to the viewing audience.

Re-call: A request for shortlisted talent to audition again before the final decision is made. Also known as a call-back.

Release form: A document signed by the performer, giving permission for all photographic, video and audio footage to be used as per the contract.

Roll camera: A verbal instruction to start recording.

Rolling: Term used to indicate that the camera is recording. It dates back to a time when cameras used rolls of film on a spool that physically rotated. All television and video cameras are now digital, but the term 'rolling' is still used. Also referred to as turning or turning over.

Runner: A person who performs many different roles in order to support the ADs and production office. They may be asked to do anything from taking and collecting people to and from the set to delivering lunch orders.

Running order: The sequence of the appearance of the stories or content on a programme.

Running time (RT): The duration of a show, an item or a segment.

Rushes: Raw, unedited video footage just as it was shot, used to take a first look at what has been filmed on a given day. They are often viewed as a check before moving on to a new scene or location.

Scoop: An exclusive story.

Screen test: An audition in front of the camera, which is recorded and then used by producers or clients to select performers for a particular project.

Self-tape: A video that is filmed and presented by an individual without any outside help. The term is often used when referring to a self-shot audition that is submitted online to a producer or casting director. Auditions, casting and even some jobs are now often filmed by presenters at home.

Set: The area that will be seen or will be in vision while filming is taking place.

Showreel: A promotional video showing a selection of short clips or examples of a performer's on-screen work. Also known as a demo reel.

Speed: When audio was recorded on magnetic tape, which was on a spool that rotated, it took a few moments for the rotation of the spool to reach the correct speed and to stabilize. Once this happened, the audio engineer would call 'sound to speed'. The term 'speed' was also used for productions recorded on video tape. Although most filming now uses digital recording equipment, the term is still used to indicate that recording is in progress.

Standby: A verbal call, usually given 15 to 30 seconds before filming or broadcast starts.

Striking: The removal of props, objects or furniture from the set. At the end of the day or of a production, the set itself and all equipment may also be struck.

T-caller: During a live show, viewers may be invited to call in to the studio to speak with an expert or to take part in a competition. The telephone call is referred to as a T-call.

Take: Filming of a particular sequence. A take will be repeated until the director is happy.

Talent: Term used to refer to a professional performer.

Talkback: An earpiece or headphones that allows the production team in the gallery to communicate with the cast and crew in the studio.

Tally: *see* cue light.

Teleprompter: A screen underneath the camera lens displaying text that is reflected on to a transparent sheet of Perspex or glass placed in front of the camera lens. This allows a performer to read a script or instructions without losing eye contact with the lens. Commonly referred to as Autocue, which is the brand name of a popular teleprompter manufacturer. The teleprompter is also used on some types of programme to allow the presenter to see and interact with on-screen graphics.

Titles: Rolling text that marks the beginning and end of a programme. It includes the name of the show, the production company, the cast and key crew members.

Tracking shot: A type of shot where the camera is moving smoothly forwards, backwards or alongside the subject.

Turn over: A verbal cue to instruct the camera and audio crew to start recording. Once recording is in progress, the crew will confirm this by calling 'turning over'.

Unboxing: Describes a style of video generally made by YouTubers, showing them opening various products and recording their reactions.

Vlog: An online video diary or web log that is part of a series of regularly posted video logs. It can include instruction or personal comment on any subject.

Vlogger: A person who creates vlogs.

Voiceover (VO): A vocal announcement or narration where the speaker is not in vision.

Vox pops: An interview with a member of the general public. Vox pop is short for *vox populi*, a Latin phrase that means 'voice of the people'.

VT: Videotape was widely used for recording moving pictures before the advent of digital technology. The term VT is now generally used to refer to a short pre-recorded clip often used during a live show.

Wild track: An audio recording of the ambient or background sound.

Wrap: Call used to indicate the end of the filming day.

YouTuber: A person who produces and uploads videos to the YouTube website.

ONLINE RESOURCES

GENERAL WEBSITES

529club.co.uk
backstage.com
bafta.org
bbc.co.uk/academy/en
bbc.co.uk/newtalent
bectu.org.uk
broadcastnow.co.uk
careers.channel4.com/4talent
itvjobs.com
media.info
mediaproductionshow.com
pact.co.uk
presenteracademy.com
productionbase.com
rts.org.uk

shootingpeople.org
sohomediaclub.com
tacticaltalks.com
thechildrensmediaconference.com
thestage.co.uk
thetalentmanager.com
theunitlist.com

CASTING WEBSITES

castingnetworks.com
castingnow.co.uk
mandy.com
presenterpromotions.co.uk
spotlight.com
starnow.co.uk

INDEX

Active listening 91–92
Agents
    benefits 149
    finding 149
    rates 149
    relationships 149
    specialization 149
    Spotlight Contacts 150
Audio 131–132
Auditions
    key to success 150
    motoring programme 151
    purpose of 150

Body language 22
    clasping hands and rubbing fingers 42
    crossed arms 41
    hands clenched 41
    hands on hips 41
    palms up 41
    signals 41
    sitting 44–45
    standing 42–44
    steepling fingers 42
Boom Mics 78–79
Branding 124–125
Broadcast journalists 148

Cardioid microphone 77
Career strategy
    an agent 148–150
    auditions 150–151
    branding 124–125
    in broadcast journalists 148
    casting websites and ads
        advertisements 144
        branding 142–143
        ITV and Channel 4 144
        LinkedIn and Facebook 144
        profile 142
        Spotlight 144
        StarNow and Mandy 143–144

competitions and reality TV 144
    contacts
        communication 138–139
        emails or letters 139–140
        who to 138
    goal setting 123–124
    guest expert 145–147
    marketing toolkit
        curriculum vitae or biography 126–128
        publicity photos 129
        showreel 128–129
    media networking events 141
    planning 125
    production work 147–148
    self-shooting
        audio 131–132
        background 132–133
        clothes 135
        filming on a phone 130–131
        green screen 134
        rule of thirds 132, 133
        three-point lighting 134–135
    social media
        direct traffic 137
        encourage viewers 137–138
        networking 141
        platforms 136
        regular posts 137
        setting up 137
    stand out 140–141
    work overseas 147
Casting websites
    advertisements 144
    branding 142–143
    ITV and Channel 4 144
    LinkedIn and Facebook 144
    profile 142
    Spotlight 144
    StarNow and Mandy 143–144
Closed talkback 65
Communication
    body language 22

breathing 22–23
channel 16
definition 15
enunciation 23
paralinguistics
    definition 17
    7-38-55 rule 17
    tonality 18–19
    visual signals 19–20
    words 18
recipient 16
sender 15
three dimensional 16–17
voice confrontation 23
Contacts
    communication 138–139
    emails or letters 139–140
    Spotlight 150
    who to 138
Corpsing 58

Darlaston, Sam 144

Earpieces 65, 66
Ekman, Paul 20
Eye contact
    on the lens 47–49
    live audience 49
    off the lens 49
    Science Museum study 47

Facial expressions
    in politics 19
    the world over 20
Forbes, Malcolm 90

Gut reaction 22

Hand-held microphones 77
Hidden hand syndrome 40
Hitting your mark 44

Interview(ing)
    curiosity and listening
        active listening 91–92
        maintain focus 92
        passive listening 91
    management
        guest's agenda 86
        interviewer's agenda 86
        maintain control 86–87
        nervous interviewees 87
        relatable and accessible 87

planning process 87–88
    closed questions 89
    filler questions 90
    hypothetical questions 90
    open-ended questions 89
    third-party questions 89–90
preparation 85
things to remember 85
vox pop
    camera awareness 94
    microphone technique 94
    planning 92
    pre-arrange 92–94
    purpose of 92

James, Gemma-Leigh 129

Lapel mic 76–77

mandy.com 143
Mehrabian, Albert 17
Microphones
    hand-held microphones 77
    handling noise 78
    lapel mic 76–77
    polar pattern
        cardioid microphone 77
        omnidirectional microphone 77–78
        shotgun microphone 78

Networking
    media networking events 141
    social media 141 (see also Social media)

OFCOM 59
Omnidirectional microphone 77–78
Online video content
    business-orientated 113, 114
    educational videos 113, 114
    how-to videos 114, 115
    product reviews 114, 115
    unboxing and haul videos 114, 115
    vlog 113, 114
Open talkback 65

Passive listening 91
Piece to camera (PTC)
    ad libbing 97–98
    filming techniques
        be bold 102
        continuity 102
        sequence 102
        silence 102–103

take your time 102
walking and talking 101–102
location 97
scripts
disadvantages 99
memorizing 99
structure
issue 100
lead 100
overview 99–100
simple report 100–101
Presenter(s)
vs. acting 30–31
charm and charisma 27–28
energy and enthusiasm 28–30
nervous
being prepared 32–33
4-7-8 breathing exercise 32
empathy 31–32
posture 33–34
visualize success 33
warm up 32
physical appearance
clothing and accessories 35–36
grooming 36
make up 36
sought-after 26
tribe 27
vulnerability 26
presenterpromotions.co.uk 144
Production team
camera operator 120–121
director 118–119
editor 120
floor manager 120
overview 118
producer 121
production assistant 119–120
prompt operator 121
runners 120
sound mixer 119
vision mixer 119
Prompt Smart Lite/Prompt Dog 72

Received Pronunciation (RP) 23

Self-shooting
audio 131–132
background 132–133
clothes 135
filming on a phone 130–131
filming techniques, PTC
be bold 102

continuity 102
sequence 102
silence 102–103
take your time 102
walking and talking 101–102
green screen 134
rule of thirds 132, 133
three-point lighting 134–135
Sheppard, Helen 23
Shotgun microphone 78
Show formats
filming
location 117, 118
outside broadcasting 116–117
studio 116
online video content
business-orientated 113, 114
educational videos 113, 114
how-to videos 114, 115
product reviews 114, 115
unboxing and haul videos 114, 115
vlog 113, 114
TV show genres
children's TV 109
factual entertainment 111, 112
game show presenters 110
magazine show 110–111
news presenters 105–106
shopping TV presenters 108–109
sports commentators 107–108
sports presenters 107
talk shows 111, 112
weather presenters 106
Social media
direct traffic 137
encourage viewers 137–138
networking 141
platforms 136
regular posts 137
setting up 137
Spotlight 144
starnow.co.uk 143
Switch talkback 65

Talkback system
cans 64, 65
closed talkback 65
earpieces 65, 66
open talkback 65
practising and auditioning with 65–66
Teleprompter
advantages 68
delivery 70

familiar with the script 69
set-up 71–72
speed 71
sweet spot 68
technical hitches 72–73
vocal variety 70–71
Television and video presenting
  body language
    clasping hands and rubbing fingers 42
    crossed arms 41
    hands clenched 41
    hands on hips 41
    palms up 41
    signals 41
    sitting 44–45
    standing 42–44
    steepling fingers 42
  eye contact
    on the lens 47–49
    live audience 49
    off the lens 49
    Science Museum study 47
  hand gestures 39–40
  handling mistakes 57–59
  rules or techniques 39
  talk to one person
    with a friend 50–52
    live audience 52
  up on three 53–56
Tools and techniques
  co-presenting 74
  microphones
    hand-held microphones 77–79
    handling noise 78

holding position 78–79
lapel mic 76–77
multi-camera studio 62–64
props
  care of your hands 74
  handling and displaying 73
running order 74–76
sound check 81
talkback system
  cans 64, 65
  closed talkback 65
  earpieces 65, 66
  open talkback 65
  practising and auditioning with 65–66
teleprompter
  advantages 68
  delivery 70
  familiar with the script 69
  set-up 71–72
  speed 71
  sweet spot 68
  technical hitches 72–73
  vocal variety 70–71
timing 67
types of shot
  close-up shot 82–83
  mid shot 82, 83
walking and talking
  camera moving 82
  camera stationary 81
windshields
  blimps 80
  dead cat mic cover 79, 80
  foam cover 80